LOCKS AND LAVATORIES
THE ARCHITECTURE OF PRIVACY

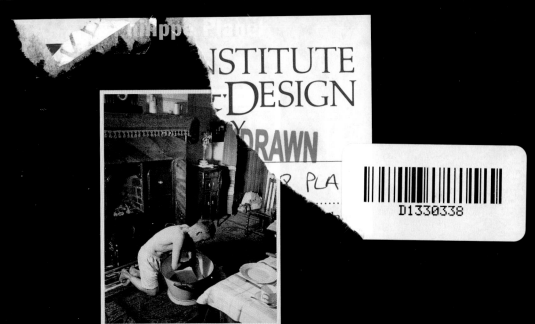

Philippe Planel

INSTITUTE
DESIGN
DRAWN
PLA

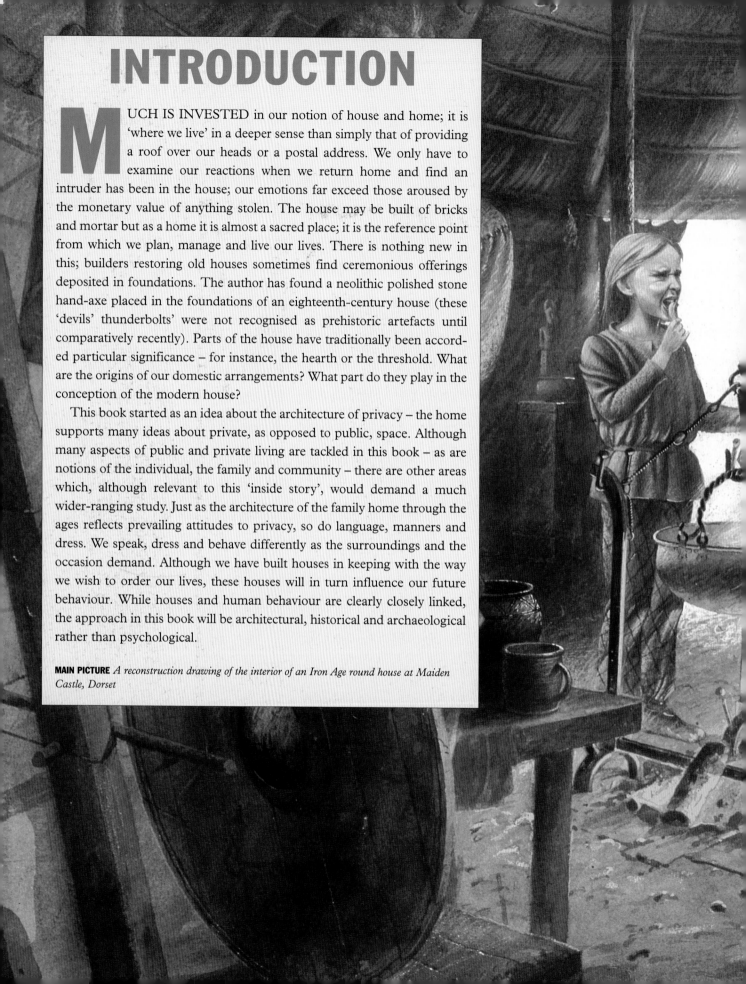

INTRODUCTION

MUCH IS INVESTED in our notion of house and home; it is 'where we live' in a deeper sense than simply that of providing a roof over our heads or a postal address. We only have to examine our reactions when we return home and find an intruder has been in the house; our emotions far exceed those aroused by the monetary value of anything stolen. The house may be built of bricks and mortar but as a home it is almost a sacred place; it is the reference point from which we plan, manage and live our lives. There is nothing new in this; builders restoring old houses sometimes find ceremonious offerings deposited in foundations. The author has found a neolithic polished stone hand-axe placed in the foundations of an eighteenth-century house (these 'devils' thunderbolts' were not recognised as prehistoric artefacts until comparatively recently). Parts of the house have traditionally been accorded particular significance – for instance, the hearth or the threshold. What are the origins of our domestic arrangements? What part do they play in the conception of the modern house?

This book started as an idea about the architecture of privacy – the home supports many ideas about private, as opposed to public, space. Although many aspects of public and private living are tackled in this book – as are notions of the individual, the family and community – there are other areas which, although relevant to this 'inside story', would demand a much wider-ranging study. Just as the architecture of the family home through the ages reflects prevailing attitudes to privacy, so do language, manners and dress. We speak, dress and behave differently as the surroundings and the occasion demand. Although we have built houses in keeping with the way we wish to order our lives, these houses will in turn influence our future behaviour. While houses and human behaviour are clearly closely linked, the approach in this book will be architectural, historical and archaeological rather than psychological.

MAIN PICTURE *A reconstruction drawing of the interior of an Iron Age round house at Maiden Castle, Dorset*

CONTENTS

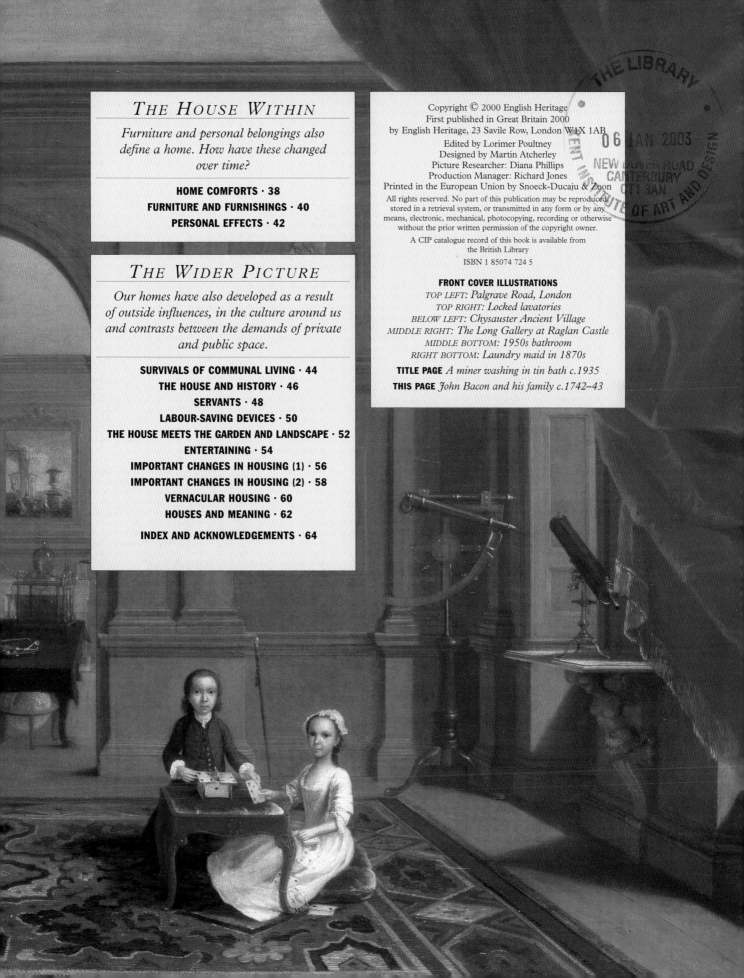

THE HOUSE WITHIN

*Furniture and personal belongings also
define a home. How have these changed
over time?*

THE WIDER PICTURE

*Our homes have also developed as a result
of outside influences, in the culture around us
and contrasts between the demands of private
and public space.*

Copyright © 2000 English Heritage
First published in Great Britain 2000
by English Heritage, 23 Savile Row, London W1X 1AB
Edited by Lorimer Poultney
Designed by Martin Atcherley
Picture Researcher: Diana Phillips
Production Manager: Richard Jones
Printed in the European Union by Snoeck-Ducaju & Zoon

A CIP catalogue record of this book is available from
the British Library

ISBN 1 85074 724 5

FRONT COVER ILLUSTRATIONS
TOP LEFT: Palgrave Road, London
TOP RIGHT: Locked lavatories
BELOW LEFT: Chysauster Ancient Village
MIDDLE RIGHT: The Long Gallery at Raglan Castle
MIDDLE BOTTOM: 1950s bathroom
RIGHT BOTTOM: Laundry maid in 1870s

TITLE PAGE *A miner washing in tin bath c.1935*

THIS PAGE *John Bacon and his family c.1742–43*

SETTING THE SCENE

How do we define a home? How do we know how people in the past felt about their homes? What sources of evidence are there? Today we regard the home as a private place, but was this always so in the past?

PRIVACY OR COMMUNITY?

ABOVE *In communities such as Chysauster in the Iron Age privacy could only be achieved outside the home*

Today we accept the layout of our homes for granted. Separate rooms have separate functions. But what creates a home, and how were homes defined in the past? We think of our homes as private places – yet in the past societies were more communal, with shared living and sleeping spaces. The single-cell house was a multifunctional space. The 'architecture of privacy' traces how the home has developed from this communal model. How have houses grown away from the central hearth to the buildings we live in today?

What measure of privacy existed for the average person in these earlier societies? We must remember that privacy need not always be defined by space – all societies have mechanisms to create privacy. In other words, privacy is largely a state of mind. For example, in some traditional societies where open houses are shared with an extended kin group, when someone turns away from the centre of the house they are effectively deemed

absent, they have achieved privacy. The inhabitants of our Iron Age round houses or medieval single-cell houses may not have practised the same customs, but such research does give us an idea of the range of responses to interiors which, in our eyes, would allow no privacy at all.

We spend much of our time indoors and if we do not enjoy privacy in our home, then we say we have no privacy. But has privacy always been associated with interiors? Descriptions of castle life, for example, focus on the buildings, but it is highly likely that all kinds of very personal and private activities, such as deals, intrigues and trysts, took place beyond the castle, on paths, in thickets, behind woodpiles and after dark, as indeed they do in other societies where there are physical constraints on personal space within a settlement.

ABOVE *The family together – 'The Family Party' by William Hogarth*

LEFT *Victorian notions of propriety encouraged separation. Here the governess is alone in her garret room*

All societies accord more privacy and personal space to their leaders, something that can be seen in architecture from Norman times onwards: the king, his family and nobles sat on a raised dais in the hall and subsequently acquired more private apartments beyond. The castle, palace and manor house were gradually extended over the centuries, each addition taking the family a little further from strangers and guests, and ultimately from servants too. Even in the royal household, however, the concept of the private and personal domain should not be confused with our own. Household regulations make it clear that both Henry V's Chamberlain and Steward were present in the room when the royal sexual act was performed. In the case of Henry VII's eldest son, Arthur, the wedding guests only retired at the last moment, after performing a number of elaborate rituals around the bed. The result of this hasty withdrawl of witnesses was a long constitutional argument over whether Arthur's marriage with Catherine of Aragon had been consummated.

At Hampton Court there is evidence that even in Georgian times the royal couple could not enjoy privacy during the night, until a system of cords, rods and levers made it possible to lock the doors from the bed in Queen Caroline's royal bedchamber. The royal privy was no more private. In Thomas More's account of the murder of the princes in the tower, the plot thickens in the privy: 'For upon this page's words King Richard arose (for this communication he had been sitting at the draught [lavatory], a convenient carpet for such counsel)'.

The accommodation in a large Tudor, Georgian or Victorian house is vast, far beyond the requirements of a family for shelter from the elements or even personal comfort. Such dimensions reveal a search for status and personal space; privacy can be now directly equated with status.

Initially there was something of a contradiction in this search for privacy since, in the Middle Ages, there was also considerable status attached to possessing a large and visible household; the injunction that 'it is not seemly that a man should eat alone' was not an empty one.

More surprising perhaps than what was happening at the upper end of society was how long it took, further down the social scale, to achieve the

level of privacy we now take for granted. By the nineteenth century, the middle and upper classes had achieved this privacy, but the rest of the population had not. A bedroom for every member of the family has only become the norm in our own century, as has the provision of corridors – a waste of space in a house, particularly a terraced one.

The late twentieth century, however, witnessed something of an about turn. Once again it seemed desirable to share space with other people, mixing the sexes in activities hitherto thought to require separate space; an exorcism perhaps of some of the residual taboos of the Victorian period. The result is mixed wards in hospitals, open plan offices and classrooms and, in the home, multifunction areas for cooking, eating and living. Freed of constructional constraints by developments in materials (the use of steel, glass and reinforced concrete), the use of large glazed areas greatly reduced privacy.

This trend appears to have run its course as architects and planners now trawl the past for references and opt for a cottage or village feel in housing and a more traditional differentiation of space – even in high-density urban housing. New housing schemes offer internal privacy (more than one bathroom per family, for example) and tiny private gardens, yet create better opportunities for rubbing shoulders in public spaces beyond, something which many blocks of flats singularly failed to do. Social contact is now seen as a matter of choice and not of necessity.

ABOVE Reconstruction drawing of Arthur's Hall, Dover Castle, showing a high table feast, 14th century

BELOW Sheltered housing

BELOW Reconstructed bedroom from Mount Grace Priory. The Carthusian Order encouraged strict segregation and separation

PROBLEMS OF EVIDENCE

ABOVE *Reconstruction of a prehistoric round house interior at Grimspound, Devon*

How do we know how people lived in the past? Our sources of information are various: archaeological, architectural, documentary, artistic and literary, but our sources are not complete. When it comes to understanding how people actually used their houses in prehistory, for example, or the way poorer people used their houses even in the historic period, sources are bound to be sparse. Prehistoric people are of course, by very definition, excluded from written sources, but poor people are under-represented in all sources until comparatively recently. How did people live in one room houses, both in prehistory and the Middle Ages? There is little surviving physical evidence, besides ground plans recovered by archaeologists and a few survivals of the tradition in the Outer Hebrides into the twentieth century.

All is not lost, however; the indirect evidence of anthropology suggests that even where single-cell houses have no physical partitions, the space within them is actually very carefully divided up or differentiated. Whereas we use walls to differentiate space, inhabitants of single-room houses achieve the same effect using the criteria of 'gender, hierarchy, ritual and symbolic association'. This indirect evidence suggests,

but does not conclusively establish, that people living in Iron Age round houses such as those at Danebury (near Andover, Hants), or at Hound Tor village on Dartmoor or at Wharram Percy (Yorkshire) in the Middle Ages did not live in complete anarchy and disorder in their small houses.

We tend to equate civilisation and civilised behaviour with more recent times; Victorian propriety and respectability demanded partition according to function at all levels of society. However, there are other ways of regulating encounters, practising avoidance or its opposite – entertaining. Anthropological evidence suggests people can behave in a civilised way in an undivided and confined space. For example, quite apart from carefully apportioning space within their dwellings, the Hopi Indians had clear rules about how to behave in a house: under no circumstances did one step over sleeping people, still less the hearth.

So, what has anthropology got to do with our own housing tradition? The answer is: more than meets the eye. For example, if we look at our tradition for male and female divisions, we do indeed find that some male preserves

BELOW *How space is organised within a Navaho hogan. This may or may not be how space was organised within the round houses of Iron Age Britain*

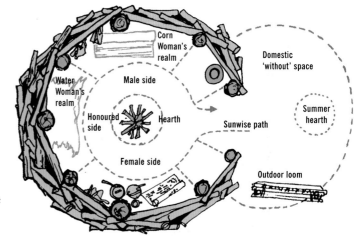

ABOVE *A scene from* Tristram Shandy – *the men together*

still exist: from the smoking or billiard room to the study or 'den' and the garden shed.

We also want to know how people felt about their homes, and while the material investment in a house can be studied through archaeology, standing architecture and inventories, the emotional capital invested in houses, especially humble houses, is very hard to assess. People from humble houses don't often write books. Occasionally a writer emerges from a recent humble background; William Cobbett describes the fond memory of his paternal grandparents' tiny labourer's house near Farnham which only had two windows and dated at least to the early eighteenth century:

> I have often slept beneath the same roof that had sheltered him [my grandfather], and where his widow dwelt for seven years after his death. It was a little thatched cottage with a garden before the door. It had but two windows; a damson tree shaded one, and a clump of filberts the other. Here I and my brothers went every Christmas and Whitsuntide, to spend a week or two, and torment the poor old woman with our noise and dilapidations. She used to give us milk and bread for breakfast, an apple pudding for our lunch, and a piece of bread and cheese for our dinner. Her fire was made of turf cut from the neighbouring heath and her evening light was a rush dipped in grease.
> *(William Cobbett)*

BELOW *Division of space in a Kabylie Berber house. The layout is similar to the long house found in Britain, but even if direct comparisons cannot be made at least it shows that the use of space is not haphazard*

The home symbolises security, safety and privacy – the ultimate refuge; hence our disarray when it is in any way violated. Our feelings about our homes and their innermost recesses are often displayed in children's literature where a door to a hidden part of the house or attic is discovered, or a child steps into a wardrobe. These doors are not fully open to our conscious selves. Tom, the boy chimney sweep in *The Water Babies*, finds a new world up the chimneys of a country house which

> ... were not like the town flues to which he was accustomed, but such as you would find in old country houses, large and crooked chimneys, which had been altered again and again, till they ran one into another. So Tom fairly lost his way in them; but at last, coming down as he thought the right chimney, he came down the wrong one, and found himself standing on the hearthrug in a room the like of which he had never seen before.
> *(Charles Kingsley,* The Water Babies, *1863)*

Even today, the way we use our houses contains much ritual concerning order, purity and cleanliness:

> Vic takes the Daily Mail with him to the lavatory, the one at the back of the house ... with a plain white suite ... . By tacit agreement, Vic customarily moves his bowels in here, while Marjorie uses the guest cloakroom off the front hall, so that the atmosphere of the en suite bathroom remains unpolluted.
> *(David Lodge,* Nice Work, *1988)*

Well-scrubbed people and houses are bequests from the Victorian period. A doorstep should be kept clean and a knocker polished in all circumstances.

> When we honestly reflect on our busy scrubbings and cleaning in this light we know we are not mainly trying to avoid disease. We are separating, placing boundaries, making visible statements about the home that we are intending to create out of the material house. If we keep bathroom cleaning materials away from the kitchen cleaning materials and send the men to the downstairs lavatory and the women upstairs, we are essentially doing the same thing as the bushman wife when she arrives at a new camp.
> *(Mary Douglas,* Purity and Danger, *1966)*

ABOVE *A Manchester housewife on her knees scrubbing the front door step*

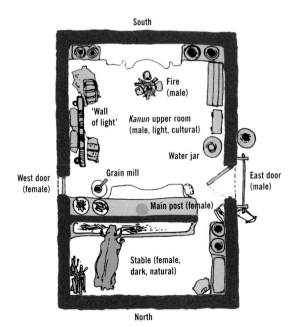

South

Fire (male)

'Wall of light'

Kanun upper room (male, light, cultural)

Water jar

West door (female)

Grain mill

East door (male)

Main post (female)

Stable (female, dark, natural)

North

KEY IDEAS IN HOUSING

When we look at a building, particularly an old one, we often tend to assume it is there because it is there, and to forget that its form is the result of number of human choices concerning position, orientation, size, internal divisions, etc. Decisions were made, disagreements may have been voiced and rival propositions put forward. Depending on the building and period these transactions could continue as the building took shape, with or without the presence of an architect.

Builders have, of course, always had to work within parameters, which is why we do not find Victorian terraced housing in the Iron Age. These parameters include the availability of materials, time, costs, technological constraints and finally, the cultural tradition of the builders. This book will largely be concerned with the cultural variable.

Cultural traditions have come and gone, and with them different house types. Roman villas were closely associated with Roman culture, while the tribal Saxons (not to mention Angles, Jutes, Frisians and Franks) had little use for them. Changes in housing culture can be attributed to notions of privacy, representations of the world, ideas about entertaining, status and propriety. These changes are quickly

incorporated into our buildings, either by adapting old buildings to new needs (partitioning, extending, etc.) or by building afresh. Few archaeological artefacts contain such a history of adaptation and change within their fabric as the older house. Most artefacts only carry information about the period for which they were produced, whereas a medieval hall house may be floored over in the Tudor period or a Georgian facade built onto a Tudor farmhouse.

If we spend what may seem an inordinate time considering the homes of the rich it is not just because these dwellings survive the centuries better, but also because what we observe in the wealthiest dwellings tends to percolate down the social scale. In the main, the class below emulates the class above and aspires to join it. Nowhere is this more evident than in

ABOVE *Medieval long house from Wharram Percy, Yorkshire*

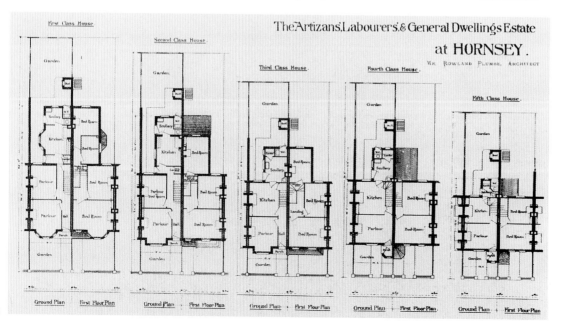

LEFT *Plans of five levels of Victorian terraced housing at Hornsey, north London. Each small difference in size reflected a difference in social status and class*

the Victorian period when speculative builders began to build for a mass market and very small differences in status were reflected in the outward appearance and internal divisions of the house: separate staircases for servants, additional reception rooms, kitchen with scullery, etc.

The differences in housing culture on either side of the chasm of class and wealth can at times seem to be the product of different societies with different values. Jane Austen's novels are bathed in the light and space afforded by 'polite architecture', while the housing of many rural people at the time, and later, was truly dreadful – in large part due to the poor wages and lack of investment of the very landowners who trip through Jane Austen's pages:

> Most of the cottages being of the worst description, some mere mud hovels, and situated in low and damp places with cesspools or accumulation of filth close to the doors. The mud floors of many are much below the level of the road, and in wet seasons are no better than so much clay. In a family consisting of six persons, two had fever, the mud floor of their cottage was at least one foot below the lane; it consisted of one small room only.... In many of the cottages where synochus prevailed, the beds stood on the ground floor which was damp three parts of the year; scarcely one had a fireplace in the bedroom, and one had a single pane of glass stuck in the mud wall as its only window, with a large heap of wet and dirty potatoes in one corner. *(John Fox, medical officer of the Cerne Poor Law Union in Dorset, 1842)*

William Cobbett, on his *Rural Rides*, frequently met pinched faced labourers on the verge of collapse from malnutrition. Clearly such men and their families had no money to spend on their hovels or furniture and fittings. Many agricultural labourers were actually worse off than their prehistoric forebears: they could not benefit from animal warmth in winter (enclosure of common land made it

impossible for ordinary people to keep animals); they could not share human warmth (because the extended family and kin group had disappeared as an economic, social and housing unit); they could not catch any fish, fowl or game (it all belonged to landowners). Yet for all this, the view still endures that the country has always been a pleasant place to live in, perhaps because the shameful evidence of the wattle and mud houses of the poor has disappeared.

ABOVE *'The Children's Breakfast', 1878, by Frederick Daniel Hardy. One can pick out the underside of a straw roof of this modest home*

BELOW *Rural housing remained poor for a long time. A scene like that in this medieval painting would have been equally recognisable several hundred years later*

A HEARTH IS A HOME

ABOVE *Reconstruction of a medieval house in Wharram Percy. Here all the household activities take place in the one room, shared with the animals*

BELOW *Interior of a 'black-house', Arnol, Isle of Lewis. Here the open hearth still takes precedence*

IN THE BEGINNING

The early house in England was an undivided, unpartitioned house with a central hearth. If there is one feature of even prehistoric dwellings that archaeologists can usually recognise it is the hearth. In fact, hearths predate the first settled Neolithic communities in England; the presence of the essentially nomadic Palaeolithic and Mesolithic population can also be identified by hearths and the activities practised around the hearth.

Small wonder then that the hearth has always been closely associated with the idea of the home – the Latin for hearth is focus. The hearth in fact defines the home, across both time and space. When the bushman wife arrives at a new camp site she chooses the place for the fire and sticks a rod in the ground. The fire is oriented to give a right and left side, dividing the temporary home between male and female quarters. The hearth has also been a defining feature of a home in Britain. In some areas, such as the New Forest, the existence of a hearth legally establishes the pre-existence of a dwelling; the hearth has also been used as a unit of taxation.

Bring a fire into an enclosed area and you have essentially tamed nature and domesticated space. The space around the fire is basically human space and can be expressed in terms of the opposites it sets up when contrasted with the vast undomesticated space outside, away from the fire: warmth/cold; safety/danger; light/darkness; food/hunger; friendliness/loneliness.

MOVING AWAY FROM THE HEARTH

If people once cooked, ate, slept, worked, entertained and rested around the hearth, the history of the house in Britain has to a large extent been the history of a movement away from this spatially and functionally undifferentiated form of living. Yet our modern liking for camp-fires, barbecues and 'feature fireplaces', even in centrally heated homes, demonstrates that we are not entirely satisfied with the shift away from the fire. It is indeed ironic that activities associated with our 'uncivilised' past, such as hunting and fishing, have become high-status leisure pursuits. Similarly, not everyone today can afford to huddle around an open fire.

Although the open-hearth, one-room house, has survived to within living memory in parts of Scotland, most of the British Isles has witnessed a gradual partitioning of the house with specific functions becoming attributed to different rooms: sleeping, washing, cooking, eating, entertaining. The house has expanded outwards and upwards away from the hearth. However, there has been a reaction more recently and a shift back to the friendly activity of the kitchen – the beating heart and motor of the house – can be observed in the emergence of the open plan kitchen/dining/living space.

Yet we do not want to live in a smoke-filled room; we do not like other people passing through our sleeping space; we prefer separate washing and toilet facilities; we like a hall which ensures visitors or strangers can initially be encountered in a neutral zone before entering or seeing further into our private space. We don't want to draw water, cut wood, or wash clothes outside, or indeed do much at all outside unless it is pleasurable and we

ABOVE *Hearth from Hangleton Cottage, Sussex*

choose to. The only exception is the camping holiday where we recharge our batteries by being closer to nature and, oddly enough, closer to other people, since only a minority of us wish to pitch a tent in the middle of nowhere. Many of our modern requirements and refinements can be accommodated on a campsite.

The New Age traveller counterculture is camping with a difference; it has identified the modern home with certain values that modern living has lost, adopting a semi-nomadic lifestyle and dwellings which are spatially undifferentiated and closer to nature and the outdoors. Unsurprisingly this has also meant a return to the haunts of our prehistoric ancestors and attempts to recapture a long-lost worldview and spirituality. The rest of us, however, have, with token reluctance, arrived at a clear idea of what the modern home should resemble. Statutory authority has, in addition, defined and legislated on the parameters within which the home must be built. We cannot have earth floors, open hearths, partitions stiffened with cow dung, bracken roofs or an open-air linear privy on either side of a path behind the house. We cannot even build a poorly insulated house or a house that does not conform with a certain and, some

would say, very limited, aesthetic. This no longer leaves much room to display cultural differences and if houses elsewhere in Europe are distinguished by detailed design features (windows that open inwards, shutters, tiled floors, basement/garages and regional roof furniture), there is otherwise little cultural difference in the basic concept of the house and its relationship with its garden, neighbours, street and locality. The next section looks at each part of the modern house in turn and traces its long evolution.

ABOVE *A 'New Age' tree house, complete with hearth (and television!)*

RIGHT *A 1960s house, where the different activities have moved far away from the kitchen/hearth to their own separate rooms*

THE HOUSE DESCRIBED

The different rooms of our homes today, such as kitchen, bedroom and bathroom, have clearly separate functions. This was not always the case, so how have these rooms developed and how have we moved from a communal form of living to one that provides separate spaces for individual activities?

THE HALL

How did the lofty medieval hall shrink to become the vestibule of the modern house? Even if the function of the hall has changed beyond recognition, the term will not go away. For instance, we still call a large house a 'hall' – like Toad Hall – recalling its former importance.

The common link between the huge medieval banqueting hall and our tiny hall is that both are transitional zones, spaces we share with visitors and strangers. The hall is the only truly public space in the house and separates the public and private domains. In the medieval version the hall was also a hub, linking the service rooms and living quarters.

The castle, with its hall and chamber, was the architectural expression of a society cemented by a bond of personal allegiance to a lord. Feudal society could not function without face-to-face contact and the hall was perfect for this role. The great stone castle keeps of the Normans often only contained the hall, lord's chamber and chapel. Later, as money and space permitted, the lord's chamber became the great chamber (in reality another hall), and the lord moved progressively further away from public view.

The central position of the hall in relationship to the rest of the later

ABOVE *A cut-away drawing of a house from North Cray. Two frames have been inserted: the first separates the entrance from the hall and provides a new chamber over the passage; the second divides off a 'smoke bay', with an inglenook fireplace*

medieval aristocratic house is as important and constantly occurring as the church in the medieval monastery. In the courtyard house, for example, the entrance to the hall was invariably opposite the main entrance and was flanked on one side by kitchen, buttery and pantry, and on the other by parlour and/or great chamber.

On the continent, the hall had disappeared by the end of the Middle Ages, to be replaced by a simple vestibule. In England, the hall had certainly, by this time, been supplanted as a place to eat on most occasions, except for servants, by the great chamber. Langland was complaining as early as 1362 of the move away from the hall:

> Wretched is the hall ... each day
>   in the week
> There the lord and lady liketh
>   not to sit
> Now have the rich a rule to eat
>   by themselves
> In a privy parlour ... for poor
>   men's sake,
> Or in a chamber with a chimney,
>   and leave the chief hall
> That was made for meals, for
>   men to eat in.
> *(William Langland,* Piers Plowman*)*

Nevertheless, in England there was greater reluctance to part with the hall; the idea of entertaining the entire household and tenants once or twice a year was slow to disappear in the countryside, though by the seventeenth

BELOW *Hardwick Old Hall, with its crosswise hall*

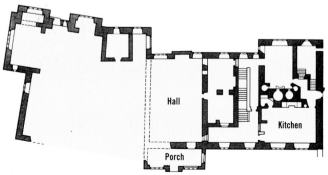

Hall

Kitchen

Porch

Not applicable

ABOVE *By the later Middle Ages, the hall had been usurped by the chamber or 'solar', such as this one at Fiddleford Manor in Dorset with its fine timber roof*

century some halls were in reality no more than huge vestibules with occasional use for games or music. Whereas during the Middle Ages the rest of the house had evolved as an extension of the hall, the hall was now no more than a module which could, if desired, be turned on itself by 90 degrees and lie across the house, as at Holdenby (Northants), long since demolished, or Hardwick Old and New Halls (Derbyshire). Here Bess of Hardwick may have been influenced by the layout of pre-existing buildings on the site at the Old Hall, but at the New Hall this plan was clearly a matter of choice.

At a humbler level, the hall disappeared by being vertically divided into two storeys as soon as chimney technology permitted it. In new house-building from the sixteenth century onwards, the hall simply became a parlour, and the huge central chimney, the usurper of the hall, enjoyed pride of place. Chimneys made the open hall house of the late Middle Ages, where the open aspect was vital in providing an upwards escape route for smoke, redundant. This change was more than a simple technological development, as the increasing partitioning of the house meant that large communal spaces and the communal living that went with them became a thing of the past.

Eventually, in the larger house, servants were accommodated in their own hall and, as Mark Girouard has

pointed out, there was no longer any point in having a great chamber above the hall if the servants no longer ate in the hall. The link between the hall and the main reception room was thus also broken. If the hall survived it was not so much because it provided space for public entertainment and feasting, but because it made a magnificent entrance to a building, and architects and their clients wished to retain at least one space that rose to the full height of the house and allowed them to show off a staircase. These two aspects of the hall are still a feature of even modern houses, since the hall is also often the stairwell and gives volume and light to the centre of the house.

The hall did enjoy one revival before being reduced to the entrance space of today's homes. The Victorians, with their passion for the gothic and the Middle Ages, revived the hall in some country houses, with the intention of also reviving the custom of large-scale entertaining for guests and what now passed for retainers – estate workers and tenants. It also functioned as an informal sitting room, a games room, a concert hall and a place for people to mingle, irrespective of sex and generation, in houses that were otherwise divided between the sexes and generations.

ABOVE *Reconstruction drawing of a royal feast in the Great Hall of Caerphilly Castle, 1326. A medieval hall was where the lord ate and could be seen by his guests and retainers*

BELOW *Pugin's drawing for the great hall at Scarisbrick Hall, complete with screens passage and minstrel's gallery*

THE BEDROOM

LEFT *Christiane de Pisan presenting her book to Queen Isabella of France. A good example of how bedrooms in medieval times were in fact 'bed-sitting' rooms*

ABOVE *Box bed of flagstone from Skara Brae*

Today, we regard sleep as an activity that merits its own accommodation, but this was not always so. From documentary sources we know about the huge retinues and households of medieval lords, but we will search in vain if we try to find separate sleeping accommodation for upwards of a hundred people in the castles and manor houses that they lived in. The king and some important barons did have their own bedrooms, but at the end of the evening most members of the household would just settle down where they could, on the benches in the hall or, if they were the lord's personal servants, on the threshold or inside the king or lord's room. Communal or dormitory arrangements extended even to knights – the knights' chamber. Royal scullions were still sleeping on the kitchen floor in the sixteenth century.

The early Norman kings and lords (including bishops) did not separate eating, entertaining and sleeping, and the lord's chamber was used for all of these functions. In time, however, the lord retreated from the public domain. For example, Rochester Castle (Kent), built by the Archbishops of Canterbury in the early twelfth century, has one of the first double chambers, separating the accomodation between day-time and night-time use.

In the following century, the lord retreated even further from public gaze. At Conisbrough Castle in Yorkshire, with its great tower, the retreat was upwards to a bedchamber at the top of the tower. The hall was in the courtyard below. This separation has more to do with sleeping than eating, as the latter remained a communal activity for much longer. When the lord's chamber became too public, he retreated into a further room, sometimes called the privy chamber, though a bed was left in the great chamber as a kind of evolutionary relic.

Throughout the Middle Ages, bedrooms should be more correctly thought of as bed-sitting rooms; they could also be used for eating and receiving guests. Gradually the number of rooms increased, as did apartments consisting of paired rooms (inner and outer), usually known as 'lodgings'. The need to provide more of these rooms often resulted in the courtyard and collegiate plan (see page 44). Lodgings could themselves be divided into inner and outer chambers,

ABOVE *The great chamber, with the hall beyond, in the keep of Rochester Castle*

the lord's wife often occupying the inner chamber.

Even though the provision of separate areas for sleep grew, sleep was still not a private activity. The 'pallet chamber' meant that servants would put down sleeping pallets at night (at least two servants to a pallet). It would be centuries before lords escaped from the attention of their servants, but they were partly there to prevent their lords receiving unwanted guests. Strange things could happen under the cover of darkness, only partially relieved by inadequate lighting; identities could be confused and the only way servants could guarantee their lord's security was physically to block access to the lord's bedchamber.

For many centuries, well beyond the Middle Ages, beds were the only warm and draught-free places in houses. As a consequence, they were used both during the day and night, and not solely for sleeping. Boswell records the young Samuel Johnson's memories of time spent in his mother's bed. Nor should we expect to find one person to a bed or one or two people to a bedroom: in *The Vicar of Wakefield* Goldsmith's Reverend Primrose describes his home:

> My house consisted of but one storey, and was covered with thatch, which gave it an air of great snugness ... Though the same room served us for parlour and kitchen that only made it warmer. There were three other apartments – one for my wife and me; another for our two daughters within our room; and the third with two beds for the rest of the children.
> *(Oliver Goldsmith,* The Vicar of Wakefield, *1766)*

We can only guess at how the two daughters contrived to have a separate 'apartment' within the parents' room, which could hardly have been soundproof, or for that matter how many children are included in the phrase 'the rest of the children'. Even in the eighteenth century, sleep was not a private activity. We should not be surprised then to find this reflected in architecture; even in fine Georgian houses, there are bedrooms that can only be reached through other bedrooms, since the corridor was a device

only used sparingly. Were readers of *Vanity Fair* shocked that Betty Sharp was, on her first night at Sir Pitt Crawley's town house, 'made to pass the night in an old gloomy bed, and by the side of an old gloomy charwoman'? Even in the early twentieth century, in the smaller terraced house, the back bedroom could often only be reached through another bedroom.

Charles II had to suffer visitors in his bedroom, but he seems to have suffered them gladly since even the commoner, John Evelyn, was received there. At the other end of the social scale, the inhabitants of single-room rural houses had no bedroom as such and draughts were kept at bay by the box bed. A measure of privacy was achieved by thus enclosing the bed in a wooden shell – the same principle as the canopy in the higher-status four-poster bed.

Today the bed is all things to all men and all women, whether it be filled with water, close to the ground (futon), antique or near the ceiling (bunk bed); the bedroom is clearly partitioned off as private space and only used to receive guests by children!

ABOVE *Chinese Chippendale style bed from Badminton House, mid-eighteenth century. The curtains both provided privacy and kept out the draughts*

ABOVE *The 'Great Bed of Ware', a huge bed from one of the town's inns that could hold several people at one time*

TOP *A cupboard-bed in Kennixton Farmhouse, Llangennydd, now in the Welsh Folk Museum*

LEFT *Bed-cupboard from Badenoch, Scotland, dated 1702*

17

RECEPTION ROOMS

Receiving guests has a prehistory as well as a history, and is archaeologically recognisable within the Iron Age round house and the Anglo-Saxon hall, emerging more clearly in the surviving buildings of the Middle Ages. The medieval hall was the reception room par excellence: the lord sat on a dais with his family and showed his public face to guests, tenants and servants.

By the mid-fourteenth century, however, lords no longer ate in the hall except on formal occasions, preferring the great chamber which could also serve as a bedchamber. Smaller rooms also contained beds and they too could be used for receiving guests in a more intimate fashion. The particular use to which a multi-purpose room was put was decided by ritual and ceremonial – this was the only way the single-room house could be transformed into a reception room. As reception rooms became more numerous in each house, so the ritual element decreased in importance. It became possible to differentiate reception rooms according to status and gender. In the romance of *Guy de Warwick*: 'Knights sat in the hall, Ladies in the chamber all'. This division of reception rooms was not new: archaeology has revealed differentiation according to gender in some Iron Age round houses and the men's house or women's house is also encountered in the architecture of traditional societies.

Some reception rooms have a complicated history. The privy chamber, as the name suggest, started life as a chamber between the lord's bedroom and the privy, then became the bedroom and finally a private reception room. The evolution of the parlour brings us even closer to the modern living-room or drawing room. The word derives from the French *parler* (to talk) and their original use for receiving guests at monasteries confirmed their principal function as reception rooms. Parlours were often on the ground floor, beneath the hall, and tended to be small and snug; cold weather may have made families use smaller rooms in winter. Parlours already existed in the late Middle Ages and inventories listing the furniture in these rooms reveal the customary ambivalence concerning eating, sleeping and receiving guests. However, these same inventories also confirm the demise of the hall in the poverty of furniture, fittings and possessions recorded in the hall as compared to the parlour.

In noble households, when royal guests or guests of superior status came to stay, the lord either gave over his own reception rooms and bedchamber to the visitor or ensured that there was a duplicate set of accommo-

ABOVE *Reconstruction of Bess of Hardwick dining in style in the Hill Great Chamber of her house of Hardwick Old Hall*

BELOW *The parlour at Haddon Hall, a cosy room beneath the great chamber*

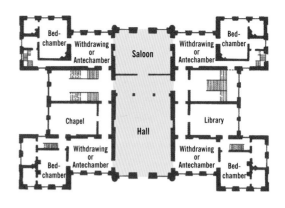

ABOVE RIGHT *Painting of John Middleton and his family in his drawing room, c.1796–97*

dation in the house; though this does not explain all instances where houses had two halls or two great chambers. The need to provide a greater range of reception rooms and sleeping accommodation explains the piecemeal growth of the noble house outwards, often within the confines of castle walls. Eventually, when defences were no longer required, great houses were planned, and were in effect organised, around their reception rooms.

The great chamber, often the centre of the house, might also be called the dining chamber, and further differentiation of reception rooms appeared with 'withdrawing' chambers, which eventually became the drawing room. The saloon has a slightly different history; derived from the French *salon*, which in France had replaced the hall. The saloon was brought to our shores by returning exiled aristocrats in the late seventeenth century and usurped the increasingly redundant great chamber. Few early Tudor reception rooms survive because most of them were not considered large enough by succeeding generations. Another French import was the 'enfilade' of reception rooms along which a guest proceeded: hall or saloon; ante-room; withdrawing room; bedroom. The status equation was balanced by the respective distances the guest penetrated and the host emerged.

By the eighteenth century, the conflicting demands of receiving guests on the one hand and privacy on the other had created houses that permitted freer movement through the use of corridors and the freedom to meet or avoid other people. The 'assemblies' favoured by 'polite society' also made new demands on reception rooms, since all kinds of activity, from dancing to playing cards had to be catered for. Bedrooms no longer had any place in

this arrangement and were exiled upstairs leaving the whole of the ground floor devoted to reception rooms.

Although the above is, in essence, the layout of many houses today, circulation is difficult to achieve in the smaller house, especially when the one reception room continues to have other functions. The number of reception rooms in Victorian houses was in the proportion of one reception room to two or three bedrooms in all but the smallest houses. The six- or seven-room terraced house was therefore an important threshold in that there could be a dining-room as well as a parlour. But the largely unused 'front parlour' in smaller Victorian houses was an attempt to create separation in too small a space.

Refreshingly, the modern house makes full use of all its rooms, regardless of size; indeed the 'reception room', beloved of estate agents, has become something of a misnomer, since for most people the main reception room is simply the living room. In slightly larger houses, formality only lingers in the dining-room or dining area, the only part of the house which may not be in everyday use.

BELOW *A typical middle-class Victorian 'front parlour'*

19

THE KITCHEN

In the single-room house, the kitchen was also the bedroom and living-room. In the same way as the buildings of the medieval castle and manor house moved outwards from the hall, so the ordinary house moved outwards, and upwards, from the kitchen. The investigation of deserted medieval villages during the last thirty years has revealed the ground plans of many single- and double-room peasant houses or 'cots'. The flimsy nature of these buildings means that only the most meticulous excavation produces any results; sometimes the only evidence for the house is the slightly lower level of the interior, due to regular sweeping. More prosperous conditions produced the longhouse, initially thought to be native only to the West. Life in these houses revolved around the main room which was, among other activities, where food was cooked and eaten.

In England and Wales very few one-room houses have been built in recent centuries, an exception being the terraced colliery houses of the North-East, called 'singles'. We therefore have to look at rural housing in Scotland and Ireland to see how central the kitchen was to the rest of the house and how, even with extensions and partitions, the smaller house revolved around the kitchen.

This central role for the kitchen is less obvious in the development of the terraced house, which could only be extended to the back and upwards. Yet even in working-class terraced houses the kitchen was very much the centre of the home and in many terraced houses neither the front room nor, in some cases, the front door, received

much use. The kitchen was always the most convivial room of the house because it witnessed the most intense activity and of course generated the most heat. In smaller houses, in both town and country, it was the room that underwent the least change between the Middle Ages and the twentieth century.

By the mid-nineteenth century, the kitchen had expanded into the scullery in larger terraced houses, where some at least of the traditional jobs of the kitchen, even sometimes the cooking (this was where the first gas cookers were installed), were done. In the modest terraced house and country cottage the kitchen was also the dining room and the living room, the front parlour being reserved for special visitors and the dead. In larger houses the kitchen was also a dining room and living room, but only for servants.

In aristocratic residences the kitchen, far from being the centre of the house, was placed at some distance from the house, due to the risk of fire. The medieval lord sitting in his hall invariably looked down from the elevated position on his dais at three entrances into the far end of the hall. Left and right were the pantry and the buttery, while the larger central entrance led along a passage, across a courtyard and into the kitchens.

These lordly kitchens were vast, partly to give due importance to this important aspect of the ritual of medieval life (cooking), but space and height were also needed to evacuate the intense heat, smoke and smell from the huge open fireplaces.

ABOVE Blackhouse on the Isle of Skye, 1850s. The single pot over the central hearth is the centre of activity in this one-room home

BELOW Kitchens of large houses were always hot and smelly places. Reconstruction drawing by Ivan Lapper of the kitchen at Kenilworth Castle in Tudor times

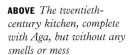

ABOVE *The twentieth-century kitchen, complete with Aga, but without any smells or mess*

The food may have left these kitchens piping hot, but once it had crossed the courtyard, proceeded down the passage between the buttery and the pantry, worked its way around the screen of the screens passage (installed from the fifteenth century onwards, blocking off the bottom end of the hall) and was, finally, delayed by all the ritual of serving, eaten, it would have been stone cold – something not included in the 'medieval banquets' of our own day! Later kitchens could be connected to the house by a tunnel, but it was not until Victorian times that the kitchen was finally reconciled with the house itself, by which time more of the cooking was done in ovens. Cooking smells remained a problem when kitchens were placed in the basements of large terraced houses. The Victorians

were proud of their technological expertise in the kitchen, though little of it was labour-saving. Ventilation and refridgeration would have to wait until the twentieth century.

After the Second World War, the 'American kitchen' became the benchmark for kitchens. This was innovatory on technological rather than aesthetic grounds, but it gave a new lease of life to the kitchen as an important room. By the 1970s, spending on the kitchen had taken off, and the 'fitted' kitchen has now become almost obligatory. Today we spend more on kitchens and bathrooms than on any other room in the house. The kitchen has become the shrine to the most recent and most unobtrusive technology: the smell, the elbow grease and the bustle are a thing of the past.

ABOVE *Kitchen at Ram Hall, 1892. Here cooking had to take place alongside the laundry*

BATHROOM AND WASHROOM

Bathing or washing in a separate room is a sophisticated notion in the history of domestic interiors in Britain. Such facilities existed in Roman Britain, but these refinements had to await the birth of another empire, the British Empire, before they were seen again on anything but a very restricted scale.

The first recorded post-Roman bathrooms are the royal bathrooms at Westminster dating to the mid-fourteenth century. Even so, wooden baths could always be placed in apartments when required, often under a tent, and provided with sponges and cloth. Was it surprise that made Seigneur de Gruuthuse comment, on visiting Edward IV's court, that in 'the iiird chamber was ordained a bayne

ABOVE *Bathing for the rich in medieval times. Illustration of the story of Sir Gawain and the Green Knight*

or ii which were covered with tentes of whyt cloths'? He and the Lord Chamberlain of England 'went both together to the bayne ... as long as was their pleasure'.

Pleasure and bathing have long been associated, to such an extent that the public baths in medieval towns, 'stews', became synonymous with brothels. Both the Reformation and Counter-Reformation dealt heavy blows to communal bathing, to which keeping clean was perhaps fairly incidental. In the meantime, baths resembling Turkish baths seem to have enjoyed some success in Tudor royal palaces and houses. At Beaulieu there were deal boards and floors with holes, forms, ladders and trussing beds. At Whitehall a sunken bath has been found in association with a green glazed stove. Henry VIII's 'bayne towere' at Hampton Court boasted a wooden bath attached to the wall, while a charcoal-fed boiler in the next room provided hot water to the bath taps. Even when provided, bathing was still viewed with some suspicion: Henry VIII was a little sceptical, and never took baths during outbreaks of the sweating sickness.

By the eighteenth century, while the technology existed to install bathrooms in larger houses for those who wanted them there was little inclination to do so since the benefits of washing or bathing had yet to be established. The taking of cold baths eventually became popular, for medical reasons; but these were not bathrooms as we understand them. Indeed, since no hot water was required, these cold baths were often installed in the grounds some way from the house; the outside variety were sometimes more like swimming-pools than baths. A few hot and cold baths were installed in the basement of the largest houses in the eighteenth century; the 'bagnio' at Blenheim, for example.

By the early nineteenth century what we would recognise as bathrooms began to be provided at the top of the social scale; early examples being at Donington Park and Stowe. The shower bath had also made its appearance, as had a water-closet with an efficient valve system. These advances in plumbing and sanitation should not be seen in isolation:

> An English nobleman of the 1820s or 1830s, purged and refreshed after a visit to his water-closet and bathroom, reclining in his dressing rooms on a richly upholstered sofa, reading the latest novel by the light of a colza-oil lamp and able, whenever he felt like it, to tug a bell handle and summon a servant to bring him an iced drink, had reached a pinnacle of luxury which was the admiration of all his European contemporaries.
> *(Mark Girouard,* Life in the English Country House, *1978)*

If the English lord had 'peaked' in terms of home comforts soon after the battle of Waterloo, most people were still using the marble-top washstand, bowl and jug for their washing a full century later. When the bathroom did begin to appear lower down the social scale it was not accorded the status of the 'polite' parts of the house in terms

ABOVE *The bath-house at Chedworth Roman villa, complete with the hypocaust system of underfloor heating. Hypocausts were expensive to maintain, so even the richest Roman homes had only one or two rooms treated in this way*

BELOW *Eighteenth-century plunge bath at Wimpole Hall, Cambridgeshire*

PEARS' SOAP

HEALTHFUL SKIN. GOOD COMPLEXION AND

SOFT, WHITE BEAUTIFUL HANDS.

PEARS' SOAP PREVENTS REDNESS, ROUGHNESS & CHAPPING.

PEARS' SOAP, THE PUREST & MOST DURABLE TOILET SOAP, HENCE THE BEST & CHEAPEST.

ABOVE *Advertisement from 1886 showing a woman washing from a wash stand*

LEFT *A combined bath and shower from about 1890*

RIGHT *Washing in a tin bath, Ashington Colliery, Northumberland, 1935*

of comfort and decoration; in fact it was often placed on the ground floor on the understanding that the bath could also be used to wash clothes. Victorian respectability demanded that any activity performed while partially or wholly undressed should be completed as quickly as possible.

Upstairs, next to the bedrooms, was eventually acknowledged as the best place for a bathroom, but there was not sufficient mains pressure to supply the upper floors with piped water until the late nineteenth century. Up until this time large Victorian houses in London were still being built without bathrooms. In poorer households the bath could be taken in a tub in front of the living-room fire, while in richer households 'hot and cold' chamber-maids struggled upstairs to fill portable baths.

Eventually, in terraced housing, by placing the bathroom above the kitchen and scullery in the rear extension, water for the bath could be heated by the kitchen range. For those in the larger towns who did not possess the means or the inclination, there was always the revived public baths, dedicated solely to the pursuit of cleanliness.

By the 1930s the bathroom had become a place of luxury for the middle class, with lowline baths and lavatories, mixer taps and large mirrors. The Roman Empire returned, or at least the Mediterranean world made its appearance once again, in the form of extensive tiled surfaces, and people could once again enjoy getting clean, though not necessarily in the company of other people. The en-suite bathroom of later decades sent out complicated messages about privacy, luxury and intimacy. For the majority of people, the bathroom as a clinical necessity, with its bath, basin and lavatory as remorselessly white as the car outside was black, did not long outlive the 1950s. The late twentieth-century bathroom appears as the creation of a society with money to burn, time on its hands and a need to dream – with only the medicine cabinet bulging with tranquillisers and sleeping pills betraying the pace of modern life.

ABOVE *'Colour in the bathroom': advertisement from the 1950s*

LAVATORY

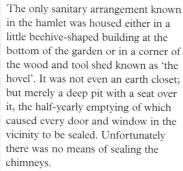

The only sanitary arrangement known in the hamlet was housed either in a little beehive-shaped building at the bottom of the garden or in a corner of the wood and tool shed known as 'the hovel'. It was not even an earth closet; but merely a deep pit with a seat over it, the half-yearly emptying of which caused every door and window in the vicinity to be sealed. Unfortunately there was no means of sealing the chimneys.
(Flora Thompson, Lark Rise to Candleford, *1945)*

This is how Flora Thompson remembers late nineteenth-century rural sanitary arrangements and is a reminder of how recent our notions of indoor plumbing are. In prudish Victorian Britain, the privy was a taboo subject and children were not supposed to be seen approaching the dreaded 'necessary'.

The Roman latrines found in forts, villas and towns are an early attempt to organise what had hitherto been an activity leaving little trace in the archaeological record.

There were also communal latrines in the Tudor period, such as the 'great house of ease' at Hampton Court where fourteen people could strain in unison.

The post of 'Groom of the Stool' is evidence that the privy played an active part in medieval ritual. His duties around a noble or royal privy included covering the wooden boards with cloth and providing a supply of 'blankets, cotton or linen to wipe the nether end'. The servant also had to be in attendance afterwards with basin and ewer, towel on shoulder. Garderobes and garderobe chutes had been integral to most castle plans and were guaranteed to be foul smelling because they were difficult to clean. Although houses with privy towers were still being built in the late sixteenth century, Bess of Hardwick's two houses, both of the same era, demonstrate the movement

away (no pun intended), from the privy shaft (Old Hall) to the emptiable close stool (New Hall).

Privies also became more private, or personal. At Dartington Hall (Devon), each set of self-contained 'lodgings' had its own latrine by the late fourteenth century. The abbots of Glastonbury had their personal indoor privy, whose fifteenth-century seat has survived to this day.

In the high-density late medieval towns, such as Southampton, cesspits were already recognised to be inappropriate, and properly built latrines were introduced, with the daily removal of 'night soil' to outside the town.

There are also indications that, for men, relieving oneself against a wall was not unusual in the Tudor period (a situation that prevails today in much of Mediterranean Europe), except if you happened to be in a royal palace. In 1547, the privy council, appropriately enough, proclaimed that 'no person of what degree soever shall make water or cast any annoyance within the precinct of the court...'. At Greenwich Palace the habit of urinating against walls had to be curtailed by plastering the lower courses of masonry and marking the white surface with red crosses. Urinals were provided as an alternative. Andrew Borde's strictures tend to confirm that the problem was a common one: 'Beware of pyssing in draughts and permit no pyssing place be about the mansion and let the common house of easement be over some water or else elongated from the house. And beware of emptyinge of pysse pottes and pyssing in chimneys'.

How did ladies get light relief? There is little evidence for the Tudor period, but Georgian ladies went to 'pluck a rose in the garden' veiled by a hooped skirt. Georgian men used chamber pots kept behind a curtain in the dining

ABOVE *People in medieval times understood there was a link between hygiene and disease, but provision remained crude*

ABOVE *Reconstruction drawing of the communal latrine block at the Roman fort at Housesteads on Hadrian's Wall*

room, for use after the ladies had retired into the drawing room. To us it seems almost inconceivable that our great eighteenth-century houses had no built-in sanitary provision, yet Jonathan Swift fulminated against any 'odious implements indoors', and in houses without internal water supply or plumbing, they must have indeed been smelly. Swift was perhaps railing at those who, like Bess of Hardwick a full century before, used 'close stools' – a wooden box with a chamber pot inside and, as one might expect of Bess 'covered with blue cloth stitched with white, with red and black fringe'.

The contents of close stools and chamber pots had to be carried through the house by servants and since odour had long been associated with disease, it is hardly surprising that attempts were made to banish such odours from the living accommodation.

In older back-to-back working-class terraced housing, the privies were often some way from the houses; there might be only one toilet for twenty people and queues on Sunday mornings.

Nineteenth-century public health reforms gradually improved provision in the large cities. By 1848 the Health of Towns Act laid down that no house should be built without access to 'proper water-closet etc., privy and ash pit'. Leeds was still stipulating one toilet for two houses in 1902, although Liverpool had already installed individual lavatories a decade before. Houses with outside toilets as their only toilet were still being built in 1900 in London. The earth closet was in fact quite an efficient system, and still has its advocates today where water is in short supply.

The toilet was brought indoors by degrees, like a wet dog; at first right at the back of the house, in the nether regions with the coal. Gradually the toilet was sanitised, aromatised and domesticated, no longer a place to enter and leave as soon as possible, and today sometimes beckons just inside the front door. Even in prosperous homes with a large number of bedrooms, only one lavatory used to be the rule; though there might be an outside lavatory for servants – a sort of sanitary apartheid.

BOTTOM *Before plumbing and drainage, chamber pots were the only form of indoor lavatory*

BELOW *A modern reconstruction of a medieval earth closet*

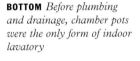

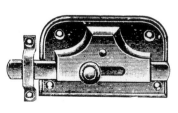

ABOVE *The hazards of waste disposal in crowded medieval and Tudor towns*

CENTRE *A fine example of the art of ceramics: a highly decorated Staffordshire lavatory bowl*

BELOW *Locked lavatories*

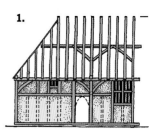

1.

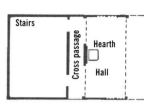

Stairs | Cross passage | Hearth | Hall

THE HOUSE DESCRIBED

HOW INTERIORS CHANGE

ABOVE *Reconstruction drawing of Hardwick Old Hall, a house that was vastly enlarged in the 1590s to house Bess of Hardwick's family*

The long history of domestic interiors in the British Isles can be seen as a search to define ever-shifting boundaries of privacy and community. We all recognise that solitary confinement is perhaps the worst sort of punishment, yet over-crowding comes a close second. The most appropriate form of living accommodation has always lain somewhere between these two extremes and is a cultural variable, fluctuating with increasing wealth, fashion, improvements in technology and materials.

We must therefore be careful how we 'read' past interiors. The fact that the Romans, like us, had a feeling for interior decoration, comfort, sophisticated plumbing and heating arrangements should not obscure the fact that the Romans were not at all like us. Archaeological evidence suggests infanticide in the Roman villa, while documentary sources reveal the sadistic treatment of slaves.

Notions of propriety and privacy have also undergone great changes. Corridors have given privacy to rooms and today we have respect for the privacy of the person. Yet, for example, with the absence of undergarments before the last century and the turn of mind of men such as Samuel Pepys, abuse of women was both simple, common and, unless we believe that Pepys and Boswell were exceptional, an acceptable form of behaviour, even in church. The only thing exceptional about these two men was that they

wrote about their sexual behaviour.

The use of space in higher-status homes is easier to chart over time. Humbler houses have either been demolished or earlier arrangements have been almost entirely swept away by later changes. There are many examples in Britain of very old cottages simply being bulldozed to the ground on the death of elderly occupants in the post-1945 period. Within these smaller houses internal space was created by using screens or curtains which leave no trace either in the structure of the house or in the foundations. The use of space, at all levels of society, also varied according to the time of day, the season, sex, age and status (member of the family, caller or guest). Homes have periodically had to readjust to new circumstances: increasing wealth or changes within the basic family unit, the departure of children following marriage, or the enlargement of the family with the incorporation of a newly married couple. Higher up the social scale, separate provision for guests, royal visits, more than one family unit, or even important servants, could become permanent features: hence large houses with more than one great chamber, set of apartments or even kitchens.

The advantage of studying older houses is that these buildings contain within them numerous piecemeal modifications made over the centuries, providing a guide to shifts in housing culture.

Some houses can be read for successive changes in wealth and aspirations.

ABOVE *Mosaic floor from Lullingstone Roman Villa*

ABOVE *Tudor chimneys along the Norman walls of Framlingham Castle*

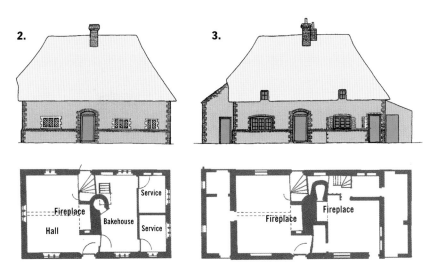

2.   3.

ABOVE *Changing taste: two designs by Humphrey Repton, 1816, showing an 'old-fashioned' parlour and a 'modern' drawing room*

Haddon Hall in Derbyshire has little architectural unity precisely because it has witnessed so many periods of building, yet it is one of our most appealing country houses, grandiose yet intimate. Haddon is also a remarkable survival because, crucially, it lay empty in the eighteenth and nineteenth centuries; to this extent it is a time capsule of earlier living arrangements.

One of the revolutionary changes in housing was the arrival of the 'double pile' house. This deeper, squarer, building style, owing much to the Renaissance, allowed freer circulation through the house and thus much greater privacy and the possibility of avoiding human contact if so desired. As a contemporary commentator wrote, 'if we consult convenience, we must have several avenues, and bolting holes ... to decline passing by company posted about by accident ... for it is unpleasant to be forced to cross people, when one has a mind to it, either for avoiding ceremony or any other reason'. The terms 'corridor' and 'back stayres' appeared in 1600 and 1627 respectively.

Each age regrets the age before. Contemporaries railed at the construction of the elegant terraces of Georgian Bath, while William Cobbett contrasted the hovels of emaciated farm labourers with the houses of newly wealthy farmers:

Every thing about this farm-house was formerly the scene of plain manners and plentiful living. Oak clothes-chests, oak bedsteads, oak chests of drawers, and oak tables to eat on, long, strong and well supplied with joint stools. Some of the things were many hundred years old. But all seem to be in a state of decay and nearly all in disuse. There appeared to have been hardly any family in that house, where formerly there were in all probability, from ten to fifteen men, boys and maids and, which was worst of all, there was a parlour! Ay, and a carpet and bell-pull too! One end of the front of this plain and substantial house had been moulded into a parlour, and there was the mahogany table, and the fine chairs, and the fine glass, and all as bare-faced upstart as any stock-jobber in the kingdom can boast of. And there were the decanters, the glasses, the 'dinner set' of crockery ware, and all just in the true stock-jobber style.
(*William Cobbett,* Rural Rides, *1830*)

Cobbett put his finger on one of the causes of inadequate and crowded housing for labourers; farmers, with their new parlours, no longer wished to have servants and workers, 'ten or fifteen boys or maids', living on the premises. (Previously only married labourers had needed their own houses.)

One of the most profound changes in homes in the twentieth century, affecting all levels of society, was the redefintion of the indoors/outdoors relationship. All the activities that used to oblige people to go outside in all weathers are today either indoor activities or activities that have disappeared altogether: drawing water, cutting wood, washing, drying clothes; disposing of ashes, waste water or the contents of chamber pots. We no longer need to venture outside unless we choose to or we want to go somewhere.

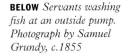

BELOW *Servants washing fish at an outside pump. Photograph by Samuel Grundy, c.1855*

27

Improvements in providing heat, water and light have transformed the activities carried out in our homes. In the past houses could be cold, draughty and dark. Now with piped water, drainage and electricity, we can mould our homes as we choose.

HEATING

ABOVE *Uses of flint, coppicing, late neolithic 2000 BC*

BELOW *In medieval times, the fire was the only source of warmth. Illustration of 'February', 1250–75*

There is a forest dweller's maxim that using wood as fuel warms you up twice: once when you cut it and a second time when you sit by the fire. This was especially true in earlier periods when the axe preceded the swifter saw. The Iron Age or medieval open fire was not fed with the regular-sized short logs that often feature in films, but with longer lengths of wood that were gradually pushed into the centre of the fire as they were slowly consumed, cigar-like. Fuel for a fire could also be procured from dung, turf, furze, seaweed and even 'sea coal' where this excellent fuel could be retrieved from coal seams in cliffs.

The sophisticated Roman hypocaust underfloor and wall-heating system appears a complete aberration in the history of heating – or lack of it – in the British Isles; a foreign import indisociable from the Roman Empire. Only an imperial system could support such luxury for its upper classes. Even in wealthy Roman households the hypocaust was a refinement, portable braziers were more widely used. Only in the twentieth century did underfloor heating once again become feasible.

Efficient and smoke-free heating requires a proper chimney. Medieval chimneys exist, but chimneys only became more common during the 'Great Rebuilding' of the sixteenth century, transforming the house in the process. The use of the chimney, often above a large end-wall fireplace or in the centre of the house, meant that the open hall could now be floored over, providing useful accommodation on the first floor. The advance did not stop there as the

chimney gave houses structural stability and the inertia of the tons of brick used acted as storage heaters long after the fire went out, providing indoor drying facilities and, eventually, ovens.

Chimneys were expensive to build and the poor had, for centuries, to make do with other ways of redirecting or evacuating smoke; the reredos being the most basic of these, followed by the smoke bay and smoke hood (the latter made of lath and plaster). These changes often led to the movement of the hearth from the centre of the room.

Even when chimneys became more widespread, and blast furnaces began to produce iron firebacks that radiated a little heat, the main room remained cold and draughty, and the rest of the house could be completely without heat. The warmth generated by animals continued to be appreciated at lower social levels, but as more and more common land was enclosed, poorer people could no longer keep animals.

Tudor mansions sprouted fireplaces and chimneys as signs of high status. A ruin, such as Berry Pomeroy Castle (Devon), where the visitor can gaze up through a building unobstructed by floors, brings home how important the fireplaces and flues were in construction and use of the house. Yet even the heated rooms in Tudor mansions were cold, especially around the walls, hence the use of screens, wall-hangings and, gradually, the much more efficient wood panelling.

In the eighteenth and nineteenth centuries, 'the cheerful blaze so dear to Englishmen' was very wasteful and 80 per cent of the heat went up the chimney. The availability of cheap coal (coal tax was abolished in 1793) provided no

ABOVE *Fireplaces could be used for both heating and cooking: photograph from Ulster Folk Museum*

BELOW *Chimney stacks rising above the ruins of Berry Pomeroy Castle, Devon*

ABOVE *An early electric fire*

incentive to improve matters. American visitors to Britain were the harshest critics of our inefficient heating: 'An Englishman absolutely believes he can warm a room by building a grate-fire at one end of it. An American visitor is in a continual shiver, his face being scorched and his back cold'. Harsher winters in continental Europe and North America had produced earthenware and metal stoves. William Cobbett spent some time in America benefiting from the heat generated by American stoves and more time, in his *Rural Rides*, berating English innkeepers and house owners for not installing them. He claims to have introduced them to England:

> We got to Thursley after our beautiful ride through Mr Leech's coppices, and the weather being pretty cold, we found ourselves situated here by the side of an *American fireplace* [Cobbett's italics], making extremely comfortable a room which was formerly amongst the most uncomfortable in the world. This is another of what malignant parsons call Cobbett's Quackeries. But my real opinion is that the whole body of them, all put together, have never, since they were born, conferred so much benefit on the country as I have conferred upon it by introducing the fireplace.
> (*William Cobbett*, Rural Rides, *1830*)

Improved grates and fireplaces, stoves, kitchen ranges and even conduits bringing air from outside the house directly to the fire, gradually made houses warmer. Central heating, through the diffusion of hot air, was first used in larger country houses such as Bowood (Wiltshire) in the early nineteenth century, while the Duke of Wellington used a primitive form of hot-water central heating with radiators in 1833 at Stratfield Saye. Central heating, one of the greatest labour-saving devices in the history of housing, eventually dispensed with droves of servants who had spent hours laying, supplying, emptying and cleaning grates and fireplaces. New houses and, in particular, flats were built without fireplaces from around 1900 in towns. Gas fires were fitted into existing fireplaces, using the chimney as a flue. However, the popularity of the 'log-effect' or 'coal effect' gas fire in the second half of the twentieth century demonstrated that the solid fuel open fire was missed – though its effects in urban areas, smog, was less so. Where open fireplaces can be retained they often incorporate an efficient Scandinavian wood-burning stove, and are now once again being built into houses, as a 'feature' and mark of status rather than for the heat they generate. One way or the other, people are no longer prepared to be cold.

COOKING

RIGHT *Cooking on a spit: illustration from the Luttrell Psalter*

Cooking has always been a primary occupation of households, rich and poor. The cauldron, and its accompanying chains and hooks, has been associated with the hearth and cooking from late prehistory to within living memory. The roasting spit has a history of similar length, while the oven covers a slightly shorter timespan and until relatively recently was linked to baking rather than roasting.

The activity of cooking is associated with women in prehistory, the Roman period and in the smaller house throughout the historic period. The kitchen in large medieval households was the preserve of men, as are many other attributes of an architecture based on military organisation. Large households in later periods employed both sexes.

The Roman period was an exotic interlude, for rich villa owners anyway, in the history of cooking in these islands. Not only were goods from the Mediterranean imported in large quantities (olives, oil, wine and garum – a refined fish paste known as 'praetor's relish'), but cooking was performed at waist-height over a gridiron or tripod.

The medieval kitchen, characterised by its cavernous dimensions and height, typically contained a fireplace for each of the three cooking processes (boiling, roasting and baking). The richer people were, the more meat they ate, and the kitchens in large medieval households were mainly involved in roasting meat, albeit heavily spiced. When King John ordered new kitchens for his castles at Marlborough (Wiltshire) and Ludgershall (Hampshire) he specified that 'in each kitchen shall be made a hearth for the cooking of two or three oxen'. It is difficult to imagine the

ABOVE *Reconstruction of a Roman kitchen. Cooking here was done at waist height*

RIGHT *'In the Kitchen' by Stanhope Alexander Forbes, 1945*

onslaught on the senses of whole oxen being roasted in a confined space, however high the ceiling. Kitchens were equipped with a wide range of artefacts for activities as diverse as making breadcrumbs to wooden or leather pails for fetching water. Lower down the social scale artefacts relating to cooking are sometimes the only things listed in inventories of poorer people.

In smaller houses where the kitchen was also the dining room and sitting room, food preparation and cooking conjured up the notion of home for many millions of people. Kitchen ranges became widespread by the end of the nineteenth century, boasting a fire, ovens and hobs. Some cooking was still done outside the house and, due to the cost of coal, Sunday joints might be given to the baker to cook.

By the late twentieth century, as food became easier to prepare, the whole business of cooking and eating was often subjected to the flexible rhythms of people's lives, with no one person responsible for the cooking. Ironically, convenience cooking and convenience eating often takes place in what are termed 'traditional country kitchens', whereas in fact traditional country cooking was inconvenient, time-consuming and involved going outside and digging up vegetables or herbs. Losing touch with local and regional

produce, herbs, mushrooms, etc. is the price we have paid for being the first industrial nation. It is many years since kitchens were supplied with wild vegetables such as Good King Henry, corn salad, nettles and pennycress, or herbs such as sweet marjoram, alexanders, rue and lovage. And, of course, cooking smells no longer have a place in the kitchen and are extracted, while refrigeration has removed the smell of fresh food that used to hang around pantries and sculleries.

Despite their technological prowess, the Victorians had not really tackled ventilation and refrigeration in their kitchens. Even when cooking ranges were widely used, roasting was still performed over an open fire. Ingenuity was instead turned to developing stewing stoves and boiling stoves; hot plates, hot closets. Even in a large household, where the kitchen was some way from the dining room, food now had some chance of arriving at the table hot, unlike in previous centuries.

ABOVE *Open inglenook fireplace from the late seventeenth century*

ABOVE *Refrigeration reduced the need to gather fresh ingredients*

RIGHT *Labour-intensive cooking was always a social activity: re-enactment of Tudor times from Kentwell Hall, Suffolk*

LIGHTING

Today we take light in our homes for granted, yet it is difficult to imagine the difference good lighting has made to our lives. The absence of effective indoor lighting before the nineteenth century dominated all earlier attitudes towards night-time and darkness. Earlier forms of lighting cast a shadow and left large areas in semi-darkness; today we attempt to recreate something of this atmosphere with candlelight dinners. Absence of adequate lighting curtailed many activities that required light in winter and also encouraged people to gather round the fire. Seen in this light – or lack of it – it is unsurprising that the open hall survived into the modern period.

Lighting is one of the few areas of house technology where the Romans did not steal a march on native developments, though their early use of window glass did allow them to use natural light inside the home over a thousand years before the wider use of glazing. The Romans used candlesticks, made of pottery, bronze or iron, and of course oil lamps, though the latter are less common than in other parts of the Roman Empire, due to the expense of shipping suitable oil to our shores.

The lack of light also meant that people visited each other on winter evenings, not so much to share light but to share company. In the countryside, this custom carried on until the nineteenth century:

> The whole troop of neighbours being collected, they sit and knit, sing knitting songs and tell knitting stories .... All this time their knitting goes on with unremitting speed. They sit rocking to and fro like so many weird wizards. They burn no candle, but knit by the light of the peat fire.

The majority of crofts in highland Scotland only acquired electricity in the 1950s, and country people in the British Isles have had long experience of harnessing local resources to light their way in the dark, for example, Kimmeridge Shale in Dorset; fish oil lamps in many coastal areas; resinous fir knots in parts of Scotland and Northern Ireland. Even the great Tudor country houses relied on lamps using vegetable oil or wax and tallow candles, smelly and time-consuming to light and snuff out in any numbers. Lighting furniture, however, was becoming more diverse and attractive; candles were set in silver or pewter candlesticks, and in clusters could also give some extra light from above in tall candle stands or even hanging stands, manoeuvred by ropes and pulleys.

The chandelier first appeared at the top of the social scale in the Stuart period, and gradually became more ornate, using cut glass to spread light throughout the room. There was also a wider use of silver lighting furniture – wall sconces being plates which reflected light. Reading and entertaining after dark were now possible.

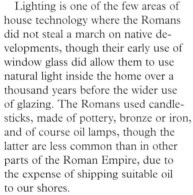

ABOVE *Small Roman oil lamp from Verulamium (St Albans)*

BELOW *A father reading to his family by candlelight, 1783*

In country areas the rush light (rushes soaked in grease) was the most prevalent form of lighting, held in an iron grip. Given that many houses were built of very flammable materials, especially the roof, and many rural dwellings had very low eaves, many fires were caused by an unprotected light. In towns this could be disastrous – many towns have had one or more major fires in their history caused by such accidents.

Candle niches were built into some stone houses, but candles were too expensive for most people, especially the better spermaceti candles (from sperm whales) which became more widely available after the development of commercial whaling in the eighteenth century. 'Burning the candle at both ends' was a means of increasing the light, but it was not until the wider availability of piped gas in the nineteenth century that homes began to be lit properly. Even so, gas lighting was confined to urban areas, often on the ground floor only, and early versions were a bit smelly.

By 1885, two million people used gas in England and Wales, by which time electricity was also beginning to be available. Electric lighting, completely maintenance free – which gas was not – revolutionised the home and the work-place, and was a totally appropriate use of electricity (unlike the use of electricity for heating).

By the mid-twentieth century, the central light fitting was being abandoned or at least supplemented by more sophisticated lighting directed on pictures, ornaments, plants, the background or, in the kitchen, work surfaces.

WATER AND WASHING

ABOVE *A water carrier depicted by Thomas Bewick*

Today, piped water is available in virtually every home. Bringing water into the house is a hallmark of 'civilised' life, and also loomed large in Roman building and civil engineering. Excavations at Verulamium (St Albans), for example, have revealed a latrine flushed by a piped water supply. However, apart from the medieval monasteries which made able use of flowing water for washing, food preparation, sanitation and irrigation, the medieval period did not set great store by plumbing and the arrangements at the royal palace of Westminster which, in the fourteenth century, included a bath with hot and cold taps, were quite unique. One problem was that the finest medieval buildings had

often been built on hill tops for defensive purposes, unlike Roman villas, and had to rely on wells rather than running water.

By the Tudor period, defence was no longer important, and with the dissolution of the monasteries would-be converters of abbeys found water already laid-on in their new residences. Even in new country houses water was at last being brought indoors from specially built conduit houses using lead piping. The siting of great houses, however, still acted against gravity-fed plumbing. Too many houses were built in an elevated position with an eye to the impression they created rather than for compatibility with the water supply. This was a trend that carried on

ABOVE *Drawing of medieval lead taps, found at monastic sites*

RIGHT *'The Kitchen', by Eric Platt*

ABOVE *Laundry at Castle Ward, with the linen hanging to dry*

unabated and various means, including donkey-driven wheels, were contrived to raise water to the house. At Hardwick Old Hall a hand pump was used to draw water up but rainwater was also taken from the flat roof of the Hill Great Chamber into the kitchen. Using rainwater was the only simple way of getting water to the upper floors of a house.

Mining technology, in the form of pumps, came to the rescue of country houses in the seventeenth century and water-driven pumps were able to deliver water even to Uppark, in Sussex, a house on the South Downs some 90 metres above its water supply. In the towns, supplying water created problems of scale and it was not until the early nineteenth century that large pumps, cast-iron mains and reservoirs began to bring water into most homes. Ordinary people in the countryside had to wait even longer.

The history of plumbing begs an important question: What did people use water for? Washing did not make enormous demands on water supply in the medieval period though, surprisingly perhaps, mixed bathing in urban bath houses indicates that washing was not a very private activity. In Tudor times, for all but royalty, washing was performed using a basin and jug in the bedchamber, a custom that was to last until the twentieth century. Bathing, where practised, took place in a tub. Soap could be purchased, as could toothpicks. Toothbrushes would have to await the Stuarts.

Clothes and bed linen were of course washed in earlier centuries, but it was a major operation, performed at irregular intervals. Samuel Pepys was clearly annoyed at the way washing interfered with the organisation of the household on a winter's day:

ABOVE *The labour-saving washing machine*

> Waked this morning by 4 a clock by my wife, to call the maids to their wash. And what through my sleeping so long last night and vexation for the lazy sluts lying so long against their great wash, neither my wife or I could sleep a wink after that time of day...[the same evening] so

home, where I found the house full of washing... [even later] the house foul of washing and quite out of order against tomorrow's dinner. *(Samuel Pepys, Diary, 11 January 1664).*

Only in a royal household was there washing to be done all the time, occasioning the employment of the only female servants in the medieval household.

The process of clothes washing created a set of buildings and open spaces which, since the advent of the washing machine, we no longer have much use for: washhouse, laundry room, drying ground, etc. And because washing took place outside the house it tended to be a very social activity, even becoming the place where the only socialising took place between servants. Today the washing machine has transformed housework, and the tumble drier has come in hard on its heels to free, or remove, people from contact with outdoors and the vagaries of the weather.

In the early twentieth century, at a time when the bath and bathroom had not made their appearance in all homes, some house owners were already installing showers. At the end of the century, water management in the house for washing people, clothes and dishes, not to mention bidets, power showers, etc. has become a key area of interest in the home. That water of drinking quality is deemed necessary to wash our clothes, fill our baths or flush away our faeces, is one of the profounder ironies of modern life.

ABOVE *Washing, wringing and mangling machine, 1874*

BOTTOM *The laundry at Pakenham Hall, Ireland*

BELOW *Washing and ironing, by Thomas Bewick*

WINDOWS AND DOORS

ABOVE *The cottage door: watercolour by Claude Strachan*

Windows and doors involve the use of technology, but they are also symbols. If roofs have the connotation of protection, then windows and doors concern entrance and departure, light and access to a wider world. For anthropologists, doors or entrances also have sexual connotations: what of our own tradition of carrying a bride over the threshold into a new house? The word 'threshold' itself is a key word in our language, harking back to a time when the daily supply of corn for baking was threshed in the draught of the entrance to the house.

In the medieval castle, technology and symbolism had to reach a necessary compromise; the entrance had to be imposing but, as the most vulnerable part of the building, also had to be defended with all the technology that the Middle Ages could muster: drawbridge, turning-bridge, portcullis, windlass, machicolations, etc. The importance of entrances, already a feature of Iron Age hillforts, the plans of whose entrances resemble bizarre anatomical drawings, was carried to its apogee in the gatehouses which came to dominate late medieval and Tudor houses. Such gatehouses no longer had a defensive role, as their many windows indicate – they were designed purely to impress.

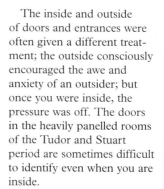

ABOVE *The entrances to medieval castles were fortified strongpoints, like this one at Porchester Castle*

But what of doors? Until the industrial revolution very few people had access to sawn timber planks (hand-sawn by two men working in a saw-pit). A wooden door was therefore an expensive item and wattle hurdle doors, lined with straw or some other material, had to suffice for most ordinary people. Examples of the latter have been recorded into the twentieth century in Wales, Scotland and Ireland. In houses built of wattle and mud even a door frame was a luxury, as were fixed hinges for the door. In this context, the wood-framed yeoman houses of the Weald with their fine door frames and doors must be ranked as fairly high in the social scale. Being able to close the door, 'putting the wood in the hole' in one easy movement, was thus not possible for everyone.

The inside and outside of doors and entrances were often given a different treatment; the outside consciously encouraged the awe and anxiety of an outsider; but once you were inside, the pressure was off. The doors in the heavily panelled rooms of the Tudor and Stuart period are sometimes difficult to identify even when you are inside.

The terraced house can only admit light to the front and back. The separate entrance hall, or corridor, where it exists, is particularly dark and a lunette or light above the door is a common feature. At the same time terraced houses were being built, with glazed windows, windows were still altogether absent in some rural single cell houses, including the Hebridean blackhouses. The use of a half door, to keep animals out, allowed light to be admitted through the doorway in all but the most inclement weather.

Unglazed windows were only good for admitting draughts (hence the origin of the word 'window' or 'wind eye'; the Welsh word 'fenestre' comes from the French). Medieval windows could be framed in wood or stone, and the larger window openings were divided vertically by mullions and horizontally by transoms. Shutters were used to cover unglazed windows in bad weather, and were often closed on one side of the building to prevent wind blowing through the house. Within the building, light could be 'borrowed' from other parts of the house by piercing partition planking.

Glass production had to be reinvented after the Romans left these isles and oiled cloth and parchment were often used for windows. Glass entered a new era of production at the end of the Middle Ages and cylinder glass eventually replaced bottle glass. But the conspicuous use of glass in new buildings and the increasing size of windows, as at

ABOVE *Example of door with 'lunette' or light above the door*

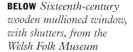

BELOW *Sixteenth-century wooden mullioned window, with shutters, from the Welsh Folk Museum*

sizes: 'The abundant introduction of light, by means of large panes of glass, adds a cheerfulness formerly unknown.' Bay windows were an ideal means to this end. When, in the mid-twentieth century, the use of glass, concrete and steel could frame windows of any size, the wall-size window made its appearance and, in its double-glazed form, kept out the cold, let in the maximum amount of light, bringing the interior into much closer contact with the outside world; although too close for some.

Georgian houses are distinguished by their windows while much twentieth-century housing is blighted by its windows. Windows are still an important cultural trait; they open outwards in Britain, inwards in France. To foreigners, our houses without exterior shutters seem vulnerable in the extreme. Does this reflect a greater feeling of security in England? Recent advertising for steel shutters would argue the contrary.

BELOW *Victorian terraced house, with bay windows at both ground and first-floor levels*

ABOVE *For the rich in Tudor and Stuart times windows, glass and light were a symbol of wealth. Portrait of Alatheia, Countess of Arundel, 1618, with the long gallery behind her flooded with light*

Hardwick New Hall, is not due to technological innovation alone; the light of the Renaissance was getting through the British drizzle. The use of windows and the vista beyond was only one aspect of a redefinition of the relationship between the house and the landscape. The great Tudor houses welcomed the light into their long galleries and chambers and, appropriately in the case of Bess of Hardwick, feminised space by bathing rooms in light.

The window revolution took some time to move down the social scale, especially since window tax (limited to houses with over six windows in 1823, and abolished in 1851), actually taxed light. Henceforth, legislation was, on the contrary, enacted to bring in more light, stipulating minimum window

THE HOUSE WITHIN

*The way our homes are decorated, the furniture
we use and our personal possessions
help define our homes.*

HOME COMFORTS

ABOVE *Woman spinning,
Orkney Islands, 1930s. The
hooded chair helped protect
against draughts*

One of the keys to comfort in our homes lies in the treatment of the inner surfaces of the house: floors, walls and ceilings. This is linked to architectural developments that gradually provided light (windows), heat (fireplaces) and sanitation (garde-robes). The moveables or luggage carried around by the peripatetic medieval household included rugs for the floor and rich wall-hangings of brocade, wool, velvet or silk and tapestries that could be hung to cover bare stone walls. By the thirteenth century things had improved: floors could be tiled; stone walls were plastered and painted with colourful decorative motifs; some of the walls might also be wainscoted, making a more agreeable and warmer surface to the touch; canopies or 'testers' over beds kept draughts away.

By the Tudor period, wainscoting had been replaced by more sophisti-cated panelling and wall-hangings, but the fireplaces of even the best appoint-ed apartments could not heat rooms to the 20°C we consider acceptable today. Comfort could only be achieved by wearing warmer clothing and maintain-ing a higher temperature around the body itself. Full-length gowns and dresses helped keep the body free of draughts. Animal furs, a material specifically evolved for this purpose, had no rivals in protecting a warm-blooded body from the cold outside the house. Indoors, what was lacking in real warmth was to some extent compensated by the warmth of the colours (red and gold were favourites) of wall-hangings and paintings.

Although the underside of the roof in large halls provided an opportunity to demonstrate the carpenters' art in hammer beams and intricate carvings, the lower ceilings of smaller rooms, warmer and more intimate, were plastered from Henry VIII's reign onwards, with the help of Italian

BELOW *Reconstruction of
the open medieval hall at
Cullacott showing how walls
could be painted and
decorated*

craftsmen. Floors seem to have followed a slower course of devel-opment, and rushes were still in use in Tudor times – carpets were too precious to be trampled on and were kept on the walls or on tables. Erasmus railed against the health hazards of loose rush floors which, given the presence of dogs and the habit of throwing them scraps, soon became foul.

Most of the features which for us define a comfortable house, including curtains, sheets and mattresses, were enjoyed by the wealthy by the end of the Tudor period (plumbing, central heating and lighting technology were late developers). Although the Romans were more advanced in some of these areas, Tudor comforts were better adapted to the English climate than the Mediterranean living arrangements of the Romans.

By the Stuart period, polished wood floors were now the norm, with some use of carpets. Although interior design and decoration continued to evolve between the seventeenth and the twentieth centuries, the only important new material or treatment was wall-paper, which first appeared in the eighteenth century.

Meanwhile, lower down the social scale, home comforts and interior decoration were several centuries adrift from these developments. Distemper (whitewash or lime wash) had long been a good standby for brightening up interiors and exteriors in humbler homes, and was also a disinfectant; regional variations included the use of red ochre in Ulster or yellow ochre in Yorkshire. Wainscoting was a useful addition to the ground floors of stone- or cob-built farmhouses lacking damp courses. Flag, tile or even brick floors were an improvement on the beaten earth floors of the humblest dwellings; though there was a science even to making a good beaten earth floor, using ingredients such as ox blood.

ABOVE *'Daisy' the first wall-
paper to be designed by
William Morris in 1862*

Even in earth-floor houses, hearths and thresholds were treated differently and the cleaning, painting and decorating of hearthstones and thresholds, in early industrial housing, underlines the symbolic importance of these features. Oiled cloths and mats were the only softer floor coverings for poorer people, but wall-paintings on wood or plaster could descend the social ladder as far as yeoman level. Stencilled designs were another low-cost form of decoration.

Comfort for poorer people was largely a question of keeping out of the draught; this could be achieved through furniture (the high-backed settle) or by an internal partitioning between the door and the fire. Plank partitions were used where sawn timber was available.

Humbler houses were often open to the underside of the thatch which, as a refinement, could be hidden by mats or plaited grass, preventing bits of thatch or turf (in Scotland) falling in the soup. Ceilings as we understand them did not exist. Where a first-floor existed, or was installed, the ceiling was simply the underside of the upper-floor beams, joists and boards. Regional variations included plaster floors, partly visible from below (Derbyshire) and boards laid on reeds (Norfolk); the reeds were plastered where they showed between the joists from below. In many areas joists and beams were plastered as well; exposed beams have not always been fashionable. The complete plastering of ceilings is a relatively recent phenomenon in the countryside, but came earlier to terraced housing when industrially sawn narrow and deeper joists dispensed with beams.

Almost each decade in the twentieth century has seen a new style in interior decoration or home comfort, with change gathering pace after the Second World War. New materials have made almost anything possible and costs, in relation to income, have dropped considerably – to the extent that moving involves near mandatory redecoration of the new home. Compared to continental practice British homes are over-carpeted and over-furnished; a function of trying to cram the comfort of a manor house into a semi-detached.

ABOVE *Embroidered cushion cover from Hardwick Hall*

LEFT *In the seventeenth century the medieval solar at Stokesay Castle was panelled to create a cosy parlour*

RIGHT *By the early seventeenth century, carpets, plastered ceilings and tapestries could give rooms the feeling of comfort. Reconstruction drawing of the Great Chamber at Kirby Hall*

FURNITURE AND FURNISHINGS

ABOVE *For the medieval household, the chest was the most practical item of furniture*

As one might expect with moveables, furniture is rarely found in-situ in older houses. At a lower level even such basic items of furniture as tables, chairs and beds were long absent. But we must not forget that in a central hearth house with no chimney, the only way to keep out of the smoke was to keep as low as possible.

There are one or two interesting survivals of prehistoric furniture of a built-in kind, notably the stone beds and shelves or dresser at Skara Brae (Shetland). Roman furniture, if the fossilised interiors of Pompeii are anything to go by, was sparse and limited mainly to low couches, tables and, in England, basket chairs. Metal fittings discovered in our Roman sites reveal the existence of cupboards, chests and caskets; turned table legs of black Kimmeridge shale are all that survive of tables.

Sparseness was an enduring feature of interiors until the advent of Victorian clutter and our own cosy but often over-furnished interiors redefined the use of space within the home. Although some furniture from the medieval period would not disgrace our own houses, these moveables were rarely in one place for any length of time; they followed the household from castle to castle and house to house. The chest or trunk (in its earliest forms literally dug out of a tree trunk) is the most common piece of medieval furniture. Anyone who has tried to get anything out of the bottom of a trunk will realise that it is highly inconvenient as storage space; hence the appearance, once households

had become sedentary, of the chest of drawers. Medieval canopied beds could be taken down and reassembled, with the matresses supported by cords suspended within the frame.

Furniture was continually being moved about the medieval hall. Trestle tables were erected and dismantled for each meal or, if a cleaner, less greasy side were required, the top was turned to reveal a cleaner surface – hence the origin of the phrase 'turning the tables'. The only furniture that stayed in one place were items such as benches which were placed against the walls. Indeed, until the end of the eighteenth century, this was how furniture was displayed, never in the middle of the room, whether the room in question was a farm kitchen or Georgian parlour. The gate-leg table had made its appearance by the seventeenth century, another way of keeping the centre of the room free of congestion. The transition from the bench to the chair, from communal or shared seating to individual seating, is itself an important one. George Paramore, yeoman farmer of Reculver (Kent) had a chair in his Tudor hall house, everyone else had 'a bench with a mat'.

As rooms acquired their own specific function, furniture could be left in position. In saloons, conventional modes of discourse and conversation became fossilised in the disposition of seating arrangements. Today, furniture is, in most homes, left in place. The position of the television in the living-room determines the position of the chairs and sofa. Attention is focused on the television rather than any central feature in the room. Consequently the first encounter visitors have with their hosts can be with the backs of their heads.

In the Tudor period a new category of furnishing appeared – portraits, including those of Roman Emperors; these were displayed to good effect in long galleries. Other forms of painting followed, but portraits of family and friends provided identity and reassurance to the homeowner and were aptly described as a

ABOVE *William Brooke, 10th Lord Cobham, and his family, 1567*

BOTTOM RIGHT *Tudor and Stuart furniture was solid and practical, useful for storage, and placed against the walls*

BELOW *Stone shelving in the prehistoric settlement at Skara Brae, Shetland*

'comfortable sight' by one Tudor magnate. Bess of Hardwick's inventory of 1601 lists several dozen portraits, including Spanish and French subjects, and one portrait of herself.

When the lower orders gradually began to acquire furniture it had to be adapted to quite different circumstances: three-legged stools and chairs, unlike the four-legged variety, are always stable on an uneven floor; high-backed settles keep one's back out of the draught. From the eighteenth century onwards, the prized item of furniture was the dresser, conventionally placed opposite the fire; Hebridean examples have an angled top that matched the angle of the low roof rafters. Here wood was scarce and much furniture was made of wickerwork, a tradition that has its origins in prehistory. Even in the most rudimentary furniture a keen appreciation of materials is evident, with the particular virtues of beech, oak, elm, ash and other varieties employed for different purposes.

Since the end of the Victorian period the pace of change in furniture design has quickened dramatically as people tried to break away from the legacy of oppressive Victorian furniture and decoration. Two important developments ensured that furniture would never be the same again: the use of new materials (plywood, plastics and conglomerates) and a wider distribution of wealth which made it possible to market whole ranges of home goods. Today anything goes, function is no longer a fetter, and materials can be made to overcome any design problem. People feel 'at home' with totally contrasting styles, and individuals will themselves go through a number of style changes in their lives. House interiors, houses even, can be put on and off like a suit of clothes. Since region, occupation and status have ceased to be parameters, furniture is now pastiche, ever-changing, provisional and certainly not something to pass down to your children.

ABOVE *Advertisement from the 1950s*

PERSONAL EFFECTS

ABOVE *Personal possessions that accompanied the dead: shoulder clasp from the Sutton Hoo ship burial*

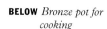

CENTRE *Teapot of 'John Ould of York, Whole Sale Dealer in Earthern Ware'*

BELOW *Bronze pot for cooking*

Some periods of prehistory, where grave goods constitute the majority of artefacts, focus our attention on personal possessions almost to the exclusion of all else, though of course possessions in death need not always indicate possessions in life.

Houses cannot be stolen, but their contents can. Keys and locks protected personal possessions in the Roman period and are even found in the excavations of humble medieval peasant houses. The presence of keys denotes a society not so much of haves and have nots, but of have mores and have lesses.

Tudor magnates, for their part, accumulated many personal possessions and, in an era of burgeoning record keeping, documents too. Lord Lisle kept his writings, along with 'a closse stole for a jacques and his chamber potte of his chamber.' If this seems a rather heterogeneous collection, the home was also a storehouse; personal possessions shared space with agricultural produce. A Suffolk man, T. Frank, in the 1570s had 9 beds in the chamber above the hall of his house; what space remained was shared with: 3 pairs of shoes, 12 yds of cloth, 2 baskets, 1 chair, 6 shelves, 6 honey pots, various farm tools, 32 cheeses, butter; 14 bushels of various crops, 6 bacon flitches and various pieces of iron.

The more plentiful written sources of this period can tell us about the functions of rooms where the architecture remains mute. Vital documents and possessions had to be secure; a follower of the Earl of Northumberland wrote: 'I wish the Earle to have in his house a chamber very strong and close, the walls should be of stone or bricke, the door should be overplated with iron, the better to defend it from the danger of fire. The keys thereof the Earle is to keepe. In the chamber should be cubbards of drawing boxes, shelves and standards, with a convenient table.' Sir William Sharington's room in his new tower at Lacock had specially made shelves for documents and valuables.

This is also a time when painting starts to tell us more about house interiors, even if the paintings are invariably portraits. 'Antic' motifs and other Renaissance influences appear in the most fashionable interiors, while in Holbein's painting of the family of Thomas More we glimpse a more traditional interior – More welcomed neither the Reformation nor the more materialist aspects of the Renaissance.

Unsurprisingly, the great period of building that followed the dissolution of the monasteries and the enclosure of common land also witnessed greater spending on personal possessions, many of them imported. Commentators such as Sir Thomas Smith objected to such a proliferation:

> Of the which sort I mean glasses as well looking as drinking as to glass windows, dials, tables, cards, balls, puppets, penhorns, ink-horns, toothpicks, gloves, knives, daggers, owches, brooches, aglets, buttons of silk and silver, earthen pots, pins, points, hawks' bells, paper both white and brown, and a thousand like things that might either be clean spared or else made within the realm sufficient for us. *(Sir Thomas Smith,* The Common Weal of England, *1583)*

William Harrison, rector of Radwinter in Essex in the same period (late sixteenth century), rails against the fashion for bolster and pillows, when 'a good round log under their heads' would do. After all,

ABOVE *Drawing of a key found at the medieval deserted village of Wharram Percy*

BOTTOM *By the nineteenth century, even quite modest households had acquired much of the clutter we fill our homes with today. Interior of house in Compton Basset, Wiltshire, 1849*

BELOW *A sampler, dating to 1795, an example of the needlework done by women that created not only such decorations, but practical covers, pillows cloths and other possessions*

pillows 'were thought meet only for women in childbirth.' People were also becoming fussy about what they ate out of: '... the exchange of vessel, as of treen platters into pewter, and wooden spoons into silver or tin.'

Probate inventories, rather than disgruntled clerics, are in fact our main source of evidence for personal possessions in their everyday context; the existence of these inventories has a lot to do with the increasing rigour of Tudor taxation. Thomas Spicer, a yeoman farmer, died in 1623. His possessions included:

> seaven Coverlettes six payre of Blanckettes, three Carpettes & seaven Cushions; one White bole of silver and one dosen of silver spoons, one Carrick Cupp tipt with silver; six payre of sheets eight borde Clothes, three dosen of table napkins, five payre of pillowties ten Towells, & one side bordcloth.

All these items were in the chamber over the hall and are followed by a list of the pewter in the hall below.

Thomas Spicer was comfortably off. John Day, a carpenter, died a century later, in 1725; he had a little pewter, 'one bras candle stick, some other small implements'. The beds in the parlour, chamber over the parlour and hall chamber are described, respectively, as 'indeferant'; 'sorry'; 'what belongs to them very mean'. No soft furnishings here.

While inventories become longer and longer for the better sort of house, the poor had few possessions . The house of a small farmer in Caernafon in the late eighteenth century was bare in the extreme:

> The furniture consisted of an old bed, an oak chest, a row of shelves for the eating utensils essential in this poor dwelling house, a few earthen vessels, some rather dirty pewter dishes, and a few other things that I could not see clearly because of the darkness of the place.

Descriptions of this sort abound but, as a cautionary note, they are not probate inventories and there may have been a tendency for both the slumming gentry and social reformers to select the very worst cases. Yet there is no doubting the genuine anger of travellers such as Cobbett when confronted with the bare interiors of the rural poor: 'Look at these hovels ... Enter them and look at the bits of chairs and stools, the wretched boards tacked together to form a table.' There was no place for personal possessions in this scheme of things, and yet this was the nineteenth century in the South of England, not the Middle Ages.

ROBERT BURNS

THE WIDER PICTURE

*Our homes are not just the product of internal changes.
Houses have also developed in response to shifting attitudes
to privacy and community, to changing social customs, to the
availability or otherwise of servants, to the popularity
of gardens and to the materials available for building.
This is the wider picture.*

SURVIVALS OF COMMUNAL LIVING

Communal life at a lordly level, centred on the hall, did not long outlive the medieval period. The growth of the state and central authority removed the need for retainers and the personal bond and personal protection between lord and retainer so typical of the Middle Ages. There are some exceptions to this general rule, however, particularly in the collegiate plan that can often be seen today in alms-houses or Oxbridge colleges. Another form of organised community – the monastery – also survived the Middle Ages, but succumbed not long afterwards when Henry VIII swept away these religious communities in the aftermath of his break with the Church of Rome.

The origins of collegiate living can be found in the courtyard plan of later medieval castles and houses. The greater wealth of the later Middle Ages and the huge personal retinues of later medieval lords led to the provision of more comfortable accommodation for noble members of the household and senior servants who no longer had to sleep in a dormitory chamber or in the hall or great chamber after the evening meal had been cleared away. From the fourteenth century onwards, separate 'lodgings' began to be built, with their own fireplaces, inner and outer chambers and staircases. Such lodgings were most easily added to existing

ABOVE *The 'lodgings' at Dartington Hall, Devon, each with its own staircase and entrance*

BELOW *The hospital of St Cross, Winchester, is still today an example of communal living that has remained little changed from medieval times. Mid-nineteenth century photograph of the Master and Brothers*

defended castle, but outlived castles and fortified manor houses, eventually petering out in the late seventeenth century for family-based country houses. The self-contained lodging, contained within a larger whole, always conveyed a certain status on its occupants and is, of course, nowhere present in buildings of lower standing. Buildings of social coercion, prisons and mental institutions, might retain the idea of the individual 'cell', even the communal hall and chapel, but the architecture and layout does nothing to flatter or confer dignity on the residents.

buildings by lining the inside of the outer wall of the castle or house with a row of rooms. At a time when other buildings were beginning to look outwards through larger windows, this emphasis on interior courtyards echoes the introspection of the male-dominated household of an earlier age.

Hospitals and other charitable institutions also followed the courtyard or collegiate plan. A good example is St Cross Hospital, Winchester, built by the powerful Cardinal Beaufort, Bishop of Winchester. These are splendid buildings, and demonstrate the resources and largesse of 'overmighty' subjects such as the Beauforts in the troubled mid-fifteenth century. The collegiate plan perpetuates the hall and lodgings plan in a number of features including the buttery, an imposing gatehouse and a separate set of lodgings for the head of the college. At St Cross, however, as in monastic buildings, the central element of the plan was the chapel rather than the hall.

The university colleges, also on a courtyard plan, feature hall, chapel and lodgings, and continue to provide, even today, what for some seems an ideal compromise between privacy and community; the public and private domains; reflection and companionship. This may be all very well if you are an unmarried don, patient, chantry priest or pensioner, but these architectural arrangements, like the earlier castle, tend to ignore the family. Since the family is the basic building block of social organisation, collegiate living could only ever provide for a tiny minority of the population – though some modern provision for retired people is clearly influenced by the collegiate plan.

One of the central ideas of the collegiate plan, the provision of a self-contained apartment, originated in the

ABOVE *Modern student accommodation, University of East London*

One interesting adaptation of a plan for communal living occurred after the dissolution of the monasteries when upwardly mobile Tudor gentry, often with court connections, bought dissolved monasteries at knock-down prices and literally hewed country houses out of the uniform monastic plan. The plan of the typical monastery was ill-adapted to their needs, except where the abbot had built a residence, usually in the south-east corner, prestigious enough to accommodate immediately the nouveau-riche Tudor owner. In most cases, the new owners acted with an insensitivity that still takes the breath away, demolishing churches that had been holy places only a few years before, or converting them into accommodation. The cloister could sometimes be preserved, running round an interior courtyard, as at Lacock, Wiltshire, or was retained as a formal garden.

BELOW *Cock Court Alms-houses, London, painted by John Crowther 1876–1903*

THE HOUSE AND HISTORY

ABOVE *Only the west tower of Kirby Muxloe Castle was completed before its builder's fall from grace*

Most houses evolve over long periods of time. Sometimes, however, houses or their interiors are the result of short-term fluctuations in political success or failure. For example, successful men at court or on the battlefield in the Middle Ages often translated their success into building. When Sir John Fastolf built Caister Castle (Norfolk – mid-fifteenth century), both the wealth and the blueprint came from foreign wars. Ralph, Lord Cromwell's Tattershall (Lincolnshire) is another case in point. Both were built in a new material, brick, which had strong continental associations. Political history intervened in a much more spectacular way for Lord Hastings at Kirby Muxloe (Leicestershire). Building began in 1480, but was never finished. Hastings was executed by Richard III in 1483, and construction came to a sudden halt.

Tudor political history provides another example of the link between political history and architecture. The 'privy chamber' was both an instrument of government and an actual room in the royal palace. Henry VII had purposely staffed this room with obscure but loyal and hard-working staff. Henry VIII, characteristically, packed it with his 'minions', or cronies, to rival the 'mignons' of the French king Francis. It was in this hothouse atmosphere that the Aragonese, Boleyn and Seymour factions fought for the king's influence. Several members of the privy chamber, including the groom of the stool, who alone could penetrate beyond the privy chamber into the king's bedchamber, were executed when Anne Boleyn fell – incest as well as adultery were said to have taken place. The intimacy of these apartments could not be closer: the groom of stool still waited on the king when he was on his close stool (the garderobe was considered a bit draughty by then): Thomas Heanage was to 'give attendance upon the king's Highness when he goeth to make water in his bedchamber.' The presence chamber and other chambers were where courtiers disported themselves and minor matters of household and state were dealt with, but the privy chamber was literally the power house. At Whitehall Palace the increasing influence of the privy chamber is reflected in the expansion of these apartments around 1530; there were now four rooms between the privy and the king's bedroom.

The dissolution of the monasteries also created new forms of housing. The bold transformation of Titchfield Abbey into a socially aggressive Tudor mansion dominated by a 'go away unless you are invited' gatehouse was the work of Sir Thomas Wriothesley, secretary to Thomas Cromwell, one of the architects (or rather 'demolition experts' of the dissolution), later to become Earl of Southampton and Lord Chancellor. Only in the feverish climate of the Reformation and the concerted attack on the Catholic Church, could men such as Wriothesley demolish church buildings in good conscience.

ABOVE *The imposing gatehouse at Titchfield was literally hewn out of the abbey church*

The introduction of Renaissance ideas in houses to England can be directly attributed to the powerful Protector Somerset and his steward Sir John Thynne. Somerset's essays in building, at Berry Pomeroy for example, have largely been demolished but Thynne's great house at Longleat (Wiltshire) survived him, characterised, among other things, by its little banqueting houses in turrets above roof level.

If some changes can be identified with politically important individuals,

BELOW *Longleat House 1572–80*

RIGHT *Thomas Howard, Earl of Surrey, in a portrait from the 1540s influenced by Renaissance style*

ABOVE *The Pillar room at Bolsover Castle, 1620s, a building strongly influenced by Renaissance and classical ideas*

BELOW *Victorian house with attic room for the live-in maids*

others can be associated with particular aspects of policy. Foreign marriages, with Spain for example, could introduce new ideas in dress, furnishing or garden layout even if this influence cannot be directly observed in any change in architecture or the use of internal space within a house. In some cases, however, changes in building can be directly attributed to these events. The return of English émigrés from France with the Restoration in the mid-seventeenth century, for example, encouraged the copying in the English formal house of the linear hierarchy of state rooms found in French houses, such as the splendid chateau of Vaux-le-Vicomte, near Paris.

Changes at a humbler level are, as one might suspect, more difficult to associate with the shorter-term flux of history rather than the longer-term changes in culture, since housing at this level responds more to function than fashion. But attempts have been made, in Suffolk for example, to link the ideas of the Reformation with the demise of the openhall house and the introduction of the closed house, where the emphasis is on self, partition and discipline. Inventories also reveal that chairs replace benches in a transition to more personal seating. It may also be that the propriety, partition and functional differentiation of the Victorian terraced house is based on a Protestant outlook and a notion of self.

ABOVE *Vaux-le-Vicomte, built by Louis XIV's ambitious finance minister, Nicholas Fouquet*

SERVANTS

ABOVE *Serving food, illustration from the Luttrell Psalter*

ABOVE *Serving food, illustration from the Luttrell Psalter*

BELOW *The butler's pantry was very much a male zone and the domain of the most important servant in large households*

We know very little about servants in England in the Iron Age and Roman periods; many would have been slaves. Even in the Middle Ages, when we know that noble households contained many servants, they are architecturally invisible. This is simply because they had no place they could call their own; they slept where they could. In the modern period, on the other hand, servants acquired their own quarters, and were encouraged to remain in them unless required in the main part of the house. Servants were no longer the 'familiars' of the earlier communal mode of living and paid for their separation in all kinds of petty ways that made the servants' quarters, behind the baize door, a world with its own pecking order.

Even in the medieval period there was a huge range in the status of servants. Upper servants were of noble birth – stewards, for example, could have their own servants. Most servants were male and when we encounter a female servant, such as 'Petronella the laundress' at Dover Castle, then it is worthy of note. Medieval servants were identified with a function and a specific part of the building: kitchen, cellar, buttery, pantry, privy, stable, etc. – the list is very long. Wearing the livery and badge of an important medieval household was a coveted position. Ladies had their ladies-in-waiting, but these, too, were 'gentle' servants of good birth, who acted more as companions than maids. Servants lower in society, in smaller houses in town and country, may have been less self-important, but they shared the medieval trait of living in a close-knit household which involved eating with the rest of the family.

Once society no longer required the physical presence of the entire household, so the inconvenience of the continual presence of servants became intrusive. Architecture responded to this new situation, and we begin to see the provision of separate stairs, corridors and quarters for servants. By the Victorian period this trend had spread much lower down the social scale to even modest houses.

The ejection of the servants from the hall, and the new servant world of the 'backstairs', is a clear sign of the transition from the human bond of feudalism to the cash bond of capitalism. Owners still could not escape from their servants, however, and, even in the eighteenth century, divorce proceedings of the nobility relied on the evidence of servants, gleaned from keyholes or bed linen. Dr Johnson wrote of servants that:

> They first invade your table and
>   your breast,
> Explore your secrets with insidious art,
> Watch the weak hour and ransack
>   the heart,
> Then soon your ill-paid confidence
>   repay,
> Commence your lords and govern
>   or betray.

Of course, the backstairs had plenty of other uses besides providing separate access for servants; backstairs also rhymes with intrigue.

ABOVE *'Washing day', illustration from 1864*

ABOVE *Laundrymaid ironing, 1870s*

Until the twentieth century, when most servants disappeared, servants spent a great deal of time fetching and carrying wood, coal, ashes, water, food, and the contents of chamber pots and close stools. There were also any amount of cleaning, scouring, polishing and washing tasks.

The Victorians, in addition, followed a moral imperative in regard to servants. As the noble residence had become less warlike, better lit and more comfortable – more feminine – so the number of female servants rose, and an increasingly 'respectable' society felt it had to prohibit contact between noblemen and female servants; this concern is reflected architecturally. At the unfinished Woodchester mansion (Gloucestershire) the male and female servants were carefully separated.

The laundry, which has been called 'the Achilles heel of the moral household', was bursting with young women. At Pakenham Hall in Ireland a tunnel from the laundry to the drying grounds was constructed to avoid contact between women in the laundry and the stable grooms. The Victorians also installed a caste system in their desire to keep servants in their own quarters, stairs and corridors. Gradations in servant pecking order increased. Technology kept pace; the bell pull meant servants could be summoned from afar only when needed.

In 1890, 16 per cent of the population were 'in service'. In terraced houses, servants were usually housed in the extension at the back of the house; this was the best way of maintaining the separateness that Victorian respectability demanded. Servants were thus closer to the kitchen, which was also often in the rear extension, and often had their own toilet facilities.

The realisation that labour-saving technology cost less than servants and a democratisation of social relationships as a result of two world wars, brought about the virtual demise of servants in the twentieth century, and made the provision for them no longer necessary.

ABOVE *'Maids of all work' by John Finnie, 1865*

RIGHT *Plan of the servants' floor at Lynford Hall, Norfolk, showing the separation of the servants' sphere of influence:*

- butler
- housekeeper
- cook
- laundrymaids

Separate stairs led to male and female sleeping quarters

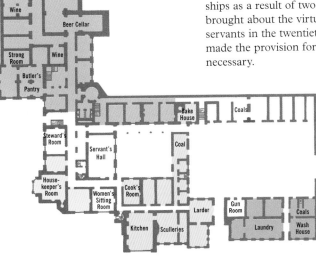

ABOVE *The bells at Erddig, Clwyd, with name plates showing which room the servant is being summoned to*

RIGHT *Group of household servants, Dyrham Park, Gloucestershire*

LABOUR-SAVING DEVICES

ABOVE *Peasant cutting wood, early 15th century*

A rich Roman or medieval family would have scoffed at the idea of labour-saving devices; labour was cheap and plentiful and, besides, being surrounded by servants was a mark of social standing. Even the high-status technology of the Romans (baths and hypocausts) was labour intensive, requiring slaves to supply wood and stoke the furnaces. From the Middle Ages until the Victorian era, society was based on the concept of service in all areas of life, and there were many gentlemen servants – again not a climate in which labour-saving devices were liable to appear.

By the mid-nineteenth century, however, the notion of being 'in service' had been downgraded to that of low-paid, low-prestige menial labour. Many servants no longer wished to live-in and, at a time of rising wages, also had the option of working in the more social and better-paid factories. Two world wars redefined what was considered dignified labour and called into question the rigid class system. The notion of 'homes fit for heroes' did not include servants, but might include labour-saving devices. This is the context in which such devices evolved; technological innovations had to dovetail with cultural change and demand if they were to be adopted.

The availability of running water in a house is a labour-saving device – no chamber pots to empty or baths to fill. But the length of time it took for the flushing toilet to evolve as an efficient device that did not give off unpleasant smells cannot be entirely explained by either technical problems or even a plentiful supply of servants; insufficient importance was attached to both washing or sanitation to inspire change. A glance at the changes in other areas, joinery or coach-building for example in Georgian times, demonstrates what progress could be made where the demand existed.

Servants may have been banished to their own quarters, but the Georgian or Victorian house would have seemed empty without them. The labour expended on an object or a process was a measure of its value; there was an element of ritual in ironing the *Times* or cleaning the front step. Today

ABOVE *Electric boiler-wringer, 1959*

we still give value to 'handmade' products, even if this factor has little or no effect on the item in question. There were thus deep-seated reasons to maintain labour-intensive activities.

Labour-saving devices depend on services (water, gas and electricity) being directly supplied into the home. Such provision could never be envisaged on a single house basis. The individual house, ever since mains drainage began to be installed (itself a labour-saving device), has only been able to function as part of a much larger, planned entity, where 'housing'

BELOW *An early washing machine, 1950s*

becomes as important a word as 'houses'. Labour-saving also involves space saving, and labour-saving devices have transformed the architecture of houses, dispensing with laundries, cellars, sculleries, wash houses and stables; they have also changed the indoor/outdoor relationship of houses and removed any dependence on the seasons – washing can now be done, and even dried, on any day of the year.

In fact, the washing machine is perhaps the most important labour-saving device in the modern home, relying on both plumbing and electricity. The appearance of washing machines in American field hospitals in Italy and France in 1944 was as revelatory as were the jeeps, bulldozers and antibiotics people also saw for the first time. The washing machine saves hours and hours of labour; more than the gas or electric cooker or the vacuum cleaner.

Plumbing, central heating and electricity can today be so inconspicuously installed in a home that a room may reflect the style and features of any period and still be warm, comfortable and well-lit. The expensive 'country kitchen' hides all wiring, piping and appliances behind 'period' features.

The kitchen started to be taken seriously between the wars. The shortage of domestic labour meant that the lady of the house had to spend more time in the business end of the home and there was now every incentive to make the work pleasant and light. Advertising of labour-saving devices is still predominantly directed at women. Technology and industry did the rest, ultimately contributing to the democratisation of consumption: every producer was now a consumer,

ABOVE *As this advertisement shows, by the 1940s the demise of servants meant it was the housewife using the vacuum cleaner rather than the maid*

and almost every house today boasts a washing machine or electric or gas cooker.

Central heating must come a close second to the washing machine; it also keeps the house warm, something that could not be said of coal-burning fireplaces, which had to be cleaned, laid and stoked. Labour intensive work is now reserved for special festive occasions, when it becomes part of the ritual to light a fire in the grate, clean the silver or spend hours on food preparation.

Refrigeration saves labour (cutting down the number of shopping expeditions), as do the telephone and the computer; the latter is also labour-creating, allowing people to work from home. Other devices are time-saving: the toaster, microwave or electric kettle. Time is after all money. Some labour-saving devices are in fact of doubtful value, these we call gadgets.

Labour-saving devices have become a necessity and we are dependent on them and the electricity on which they all run – even gas-fired central heating. The labour-saving house is totally reliant on a centralised power supply and we are helpless without it. The home is no longer a castle – switch off the electricity and it is unusable.

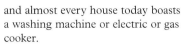

51

THE HOUSE MEETS THE GARDEN AND LANDSCAPE

In the same way as archaeology has moved from the study of individual sites to considering the surrounding landscape, so historians of building now study the house in the context of its environs. We only have tantalising glimpses of the way prehistoric populations viewed the landscape around their settlements: burial barrows, for example, tend not to be on the top of hills and ridges but on the skyline, as viewed from the houses below. The Romans, on the other hand, were definitely concerned with the immediate environs of their villas, as the gardens found at Fishborne (Sussex) testify.

Medieval castles were, for reasons of defence, social control and status, built in commanding positions, so the 'amenity' value of the landscape around them was not a prime concern. Gardens in castles and large medieval houses were small, enclosed (against wandering animals) and situated wherever space between buildings permitted. Henry III's queen had a window in her chamber at Windsor fitted with glass panes 'facing out onto the king's herb garden', while Eleanor of Castile (Edward I's queen) used gardeners versed in the Moorish tradition of interior courtyards and fountains at the royal palace of Langley. The medieval garden or 'pleasaunce' was one of the few areas in which women could have some control over their surroundings.

The medieval deer park created a link between house and a humanised landscape – a perimeter 13km long enclosed the royal palace of Clarendon, for example. At Okehampton Castle in Devon, the Eastern Lodgings, built in the fourteenth century, look across to the deer park and boast the largest windows, the most opulent fireplaces and best-appointed garderobes. The surviving buildings of Berry Pomeroy Castle, also in Devon, are similarly surrounded by a deer park; the Seymour family went to great lengths to take advantage of the position of the castle. The construction of the great North Range (c.1600, now demolished) culminated, on its third floor, with a magnificent long gallery, extending to the full length of the range and affording views over the deer park and Dartmoor beyond.

Henceforth no great houses would be built without a concern for 'aspect'. In true Renaissance style, the garden, became an integral part of the design of the house, as at Wollaton House (Nottinghamshire – 1580) or Holdenby Hall (Northamptonshire), where the whole landscape around the house was remodelled.

Formal gardens were planted with recently imported plants and shrubs, and some functions of the house gradually moved out into the garden which could offer 'some snug places of retirement' (Hampton Court), or full-blown banqueting houses. In the seventeenth century, vistas through the apartments of the house carried the gaze out into a park, sometimes as far as the eye could see; these were domesticated landscapes, not open or wild countryside, and all the avenues led to the great house. Drawings of houses no longer featured the front elevation, but were more sensitive, as were strollers, to the best viewpoints. The bird's-eye view of the house, garden and park provided an integrated view as the landscape now moved into the house in the form of landscape paintings.

The linear axis of honour of the state apartments inside the house was matched by the formal avenues outside. In the eighteenth century the relationship changed: the reception rooms of the

house could now be visited in a circular progression, so too could parks and gardens. At Stowe (Buckinghamshire) over thirty garden buildings were dotted about the grounds by the mid-eighteenth century. Stourhead in Wiltshire provided an equally impressive circuit, enlivened with many curiosities on the way.

The romantic movement encouraged a more intimate appreciation of nature, most effectively achieved with the smaller, but very fashionable, cottage ornée. The desire to possess a garden by a large section of the population, especially in the south of England, had a profound effect on house design: it gave a great impulse to detached suburban housing development and played a part in bringing the main reception rooms down from the first floor, providing more convenient access to the garden. In terraced houses it had been difficult to make much of the back garden, due to the back scullery extension and the various outhouses; but access to the garden could be improved by tidying up the back of the house and getting rid of the back extension.

For poorer country dwellers the garden was a necessity – toft (small holding) and croft (platform occupied by house and outbuildings) – are closely associated

BOTTOM The eighteenth-century gardens at Wrest Park, Bedfordshire

BELOW Vistas glimpsed through formal avenues: 'A View of Three Walks at Chiswick House', 1753

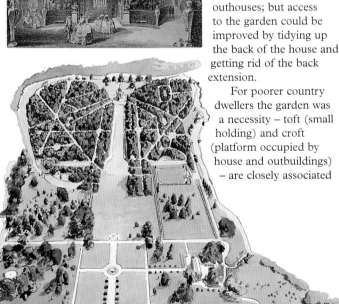

ABOVE The idealised view of the English cottage garden

in the archaeology of deserted medieval villages. It has been suggested that the narrow entranced enclosures at Hound Tor (Devon) were once gardens. Cottage gardens came to resemble a microcosm of what nature provided in the locality and since so many tasks were still performed outside, good access to the garden was important. By the nineteenth century, cottage gardens had many suburban devotees.

In the twentieth century, however, gardens became more chameleon-like, reflecting the mood of the house they were attached to: cottage-style houses had cottage gardens but modern architecture demanded a more severe, linear, approach. In later twentieth century housing estates, front gardens tend to be grassed over areas without any obvious demarcation. At the back, the patio-style garden stresses privacy and ease of maintenance. Further up the social scale seclusion is the goal, and the best houses are barely visible from the road in the leafier suburbs. House plots in England are small in comparison to those of our European neighbours, but the studiously detached house with a small garden still sets the standard. The current interest in gardens and garden centres is similar to the interest in DIY; two areas where people can have some effect on their environment.

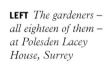

LEFT The gardeners – all eighteen of them – at Polesden Lacey House, Surrey

ABOVE *'The last scene in a gambler's house', by George Smith, 1871*

ENTERTAINING

ABOVE *Reconstruction of feast given by Bishop Longland of Lincoln in his palace for Henry VIII and Catherine Howard, 1541*

ABOVE *Reconstruction drawing showing early Iron Age Celtic firedog, from Maiden Castle, Dorset*

Entertaining displays the public side of ourselves and our homes. We are made to feel 'at home' in our host's living room, dining room, even kitchen. Should we go upstairs to use the bathroom, however, we would feel distinctly uneasy about walking into a bedroom, a private zone of the house into which we have not been invited.

In single-cell houses without partitions the role and space accorded to entertaining was no less important but was articulated in different ways. The honoured guest had a special place by the hearth. Once chimneys and fireplaces had been installed in smaller houses, guests enjoyed the privilege of sitting in the snuggest, draft-free, corner. People visited each other much more in the past than we do now; television has increased the self-containedness of the modern house.

When we examine the prehistory of entertaining we are on unfamiliar ground, confronted with a culture totally dissimilar to our own. In the Bronze and Iron Ages, paired round houses, one large (for eating and entertaining) and one small (for cooking) sometimes suggest a very specific cultural attitude to food, entertaining and gender relations. Entertaining and feasting revolved around the central hearth; cauldrons and firedogs were prized possessions in the Iron Age house.

The central public or entertaining zone of the round house seems to have been retained in the subsequent Romano-British rectangular aisled house. In the richest and most romanised households, the courtyard villa with its formal gardens provided the appropriate architectural setting for receiving guests, while the ensuing Saxon period saw a return to tribal hospitality, the hall and the central hearth – the hallmark of Northern Europe. The mead-hall, which looms so large in *Beowulf*, was where warriors were entertained, slept and fought and died when attacked.

In the Middle Ages the architecture of entertaining becomes more visible. The position of kitchen, kitchen passage, the screens passage, dais and growing importance of the great chamber are replicated in house after house with only minor variations. The documentary sources complement the architectural evidence; nobles were urged to '.. site you ever in the middle of the high board, that your visage and cheer be shown to all men.'

Entertaining was subsequently transferred intact from the hall to the great chamber, accompanied by an array of servants, including the gentleman steward, sewer, carver and cup bearer; dressed with the same attention to detail as would befit a religious ceremony. The lower ranks of the household were ghosts at the feast and remained in the hall.

The intensity of noble dining ritual included the washing of hands, the tasting of the lord's food, 'taking sayes' and the seating of principal guests 'above the salt'. Medieval entertaining,

ABOVE *Reconstruction drawing of the Long Gallery at Raglan Castle. Tudor and Stuart long galleries could be used for indoor exercise, but were also used for display and entertaining*

ABOVE *'The Dinner Party' Sir Henry Cole (1802–82)*

LEFT *Billiard room at Brodsworth Hall*

BELOW *Staircase at Brodsworth Hall*

in common with all ritual, ensured social cohesion; the rise or fall of individuals could be read in tiny changes in precedence.

Noble entertaining also involved music, dancing, gaming and plays or masques. Wealth, imagination and foreign influence (through royal marriages), pushed back the frontiers of entertaining: it could take place in banqueting houses in the grounds or high up in towers. Monumental staircases led guests to the place of entertainment. The building of long galleries inside the house, the laying out of gardens, parks and whole outside landscapes were all entertainment driven. Many of our great houses owe their magnificence to the fact that they would, on occasion, be expected to entertain royalty. For example, Audley End completely lost its role when its owner, the Earl of Suffolk, fell out of royal favour in the early seventeenth century.

Entertaining should not be interpreted as open house. The reception of guests was strictly a question of access and privilege. Withdrawing rooms, closets, parlours, saloons, cabinets and even the king's bedroom, each evolved with their own degree of privacy. Access depended on position and intimacy. A levée could be held in as private a place as a duchess's dressing-room under Charles II – though this did raise eyebrows even at the time. The growth of polite society in the next century resulted in the creation of whole suites of reception rooms through which guests could circulate. By the end of the eighteenth century, reception rooms tended to be downstairs and were the focal point of the house; bedrooms, with dressing rooms, were upstairs and private or state apartments diminished in importance.

The invention of the 'house party' led to all-day entertainment and, since marriages were no longer arranged in advance, provided the right ambience for partner selection. The peculiarly British habit of separating male and female guests after dinner appeared. Victorian morality, and hypocrisy, further segregated entertaining, with the introduction of the men's smoking room and billiard room, while also attempting to recreate social cohesion in reviving the central hall.

Lower down the social scale even a working-class terraced house now possessed a reception room. Unfortunately, the front parlour was rarely associated with gaiety; it was sometimes only used for laying out corpses, and was often knocked through in the twentieth century to create more living space. Our present attitude to entertaining is ambivalent; informality is uneasily combined with a repressed attitude towards food. Guests often receive their food ready-served; the dishes are left in the kitchen. The 'ahs' and 'ohs' as more dishes are placed on the groaning table and guests jostle to serve each other have disappeared.

IMPORTANT CHANGES IN HOUSING – 1

BUILDING IN THE ROUND

Prehistoric house-builders in Britain left little evidence of their homes, but archaeologists can usually identify prehistoric houses if they have stone footings or, in the case of most of lowland Britain, if wooden posts have left a negative impression in the ground in the form of postholes. There is sufficient evidence from above or below ground level for us to see that most houses in prehistoric Britain were round.

RIGHT *Plan of houses excavated at Quinton, Northamptonshire, where the round house is clearly overlain by its first-century successor*

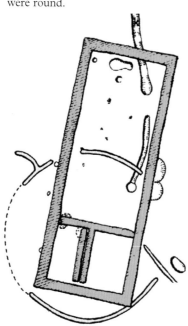

SQUARING THE CIRCLE

Rectangular houses arrived with the Romans. Indeed, in common with other trappings of the Roman world and Roman patterns of consumption, these house forms appeared some time before the Roman legions actually landed. At Silchester Roman town in Berkshire, the Iron Age street layout with round houses was replaced by a grid layout and rectangular houses some time before the Roman Conquest. Nowhere is the transition from round to rectangular more evident than at Quinton, in Northamptonshire, where a rectangular house was discovered directly to overlay its predecessor.

What does this change in shape mean? In the round house, the central hearth focuses all communal activity on the centre of the house, relegating other activities to the nether regions. The lack of headroom at the edges also directs attention to the centre. The rectangular house is obviously much more human-made; it is not a shape commonly found in nature. Benches and other items can more easily be placed or hung against the straight walls. You can also create a set of hierarchical relationships more easily in a rectangular house. The hearth, although still the heart of the house, did not have to be in the centre. Behind the hearth, one end of the house could be partitioned off to provide an inner room or rooms. Animals could be kept under the same roof, and the heat they generated retained, but they were kept at the far, lower-status, end of the house. At the lowest level in society this form was to be the prevalent shape of houses throughout the Middle Ages and into the modern period. In medieval towns the long-sided rectangle was also the natural choice, as each householder required a narrow street frontage.

Advances in archaeological excavation mean that we now know that the Saxons did more than squat in Roman buildings or live in sunken huts. Saxon royal palaces are emerging from the archaeologist's trowel, revealing a liking for large halls and communal living.

BELOW *Reconstruction of the royal Northumbrian palace of Yeavering, AD 627*

AT HOME WITH THE NORMANS

The Normans introduced buildings with features we recognise, such as the chimney or the garderobe (lavatory). The high status of the surviving buildings means that we more readily adopt the medieval building tradition as our own. Norman builders used materials (faced stone, rubble and lime mortar) which, in terms of time, effort and cost, speak volumes about the social control exercised by this small warrior elite.

The French historian Georges Duby has drawn attention to the symbolism of concentric castle fortifications, dominated by the tall keep, as at Dover Castle for example. To reach the central redoubt involved a progress inwards and upwards. At the top of the keep was the king or lord's bed chamber. High rise was high status; only the castle and religious buildings could rise above the flat social horizons of the majority of the population. The bed in the high castle chamber was the organic centre of this human hive where the feudal dynasty was reproduced. Yet, and for us paradoxically, the occupants of the bed were unlikely ever to be alone – they were too important. High status and privacy were not closely associated at this time.

Later in the medieval period, the great families preferred to put some distance between themselves and the great hall where their wealth and influence was still conspicuously expressed in communal eating and entertaining. A 'great chamber' was often built at right angles to the hall,

and on the first floor (for added warmth and protection). Subsequently even the great chamber was not private enough, and there was a further withdrawal to the smaller privy chamber, adjacent to the privy

BELOW *Reconstruction of peasant long house found at Wharram Percy, Yorkshire*

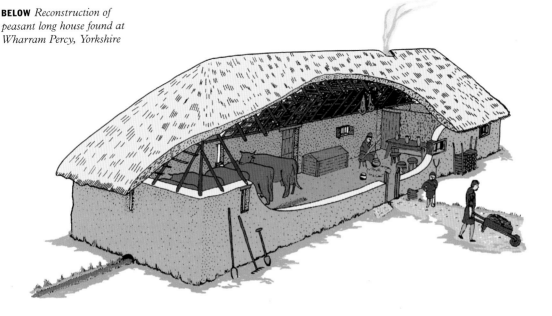

TOP *The twelfth-century keep of Goodrich Castle*

ABOVE LEFT *The guardroom latrine at Conisborough Castle, Yorkshire*

ABOVE *The chamber in Earl Richard of Cornwall's thirteenth-century High Tower at the very top and centre of Launceston Castle*

IMPORTANT CHANGES IN HOUSING – 2

ABOVE *Cut-away drawing of Pendean Farmhouse from Midhurst showing how the introduction of the brick chimney encouraged the partitioning of space horizontally and vertically*

Tudor building is often associated with the great mansions which, when built of a piece, made much better use of space than the piecemeal accretions of the medieval house. These latter houses were also more comfortable and better lit. However, the Tudor period is also the first to have left more than a handful of survivals of houses of the middling sort, 'yeoman houses'. So many were built in the late sixteenth century that this intense bout of building activity has become known as 'The Great Rebuilding'. It was fuelled by the revolution in tenurial relationships at this time. The yeoman class benefited enormously from, was to some extent created by, the dissolution of the monasteries and their lands. Everyone received handouts and moved up a step as the wealth trickled down – except of course the landless poor, who only got poorer.

The chimney was the symbol of this rebuilding and presided over the demise of the open hall with its smoke blackened rafters and the social relations it underpinned. This constituted two of the three changes the contemporary Thomas Harrison noted in the period:

... one is the multitude of chimneys lately erected, whereas in our young days there were not above two or three, if so many ... but each one made his fire against a reredos in the hall, where he dined and dressed his meat ... the second is the great amendment of lodging.
(Thomas Harrison, 1601)

At yeoman level and above, the medieval linear three-part form of kitchen, hall and chamber house gradually compressed itself, sprouted a central chimney and, in keeping with Renaissance influence, acquired depth, finally emerging as the Georgian double-pile house. Sometimes referred to as the compact house, the double-pile house was an antidote to houses which 'spread the housing too much, and a very commendable conduct to compose it more orderly together'. The same commentator, Roger North, writing in the late seventeenth century also listed some of the disadvantages of the compact house, which could be so compact as to be 'lay'd on an heap like a wasps-nest ... all the noises of an house are heard every where ... all smells that offend, are a nuisance to all rooms'. There were, it is true, other problems too; for example, all ceilings were necessarily the same height, whether the room was large or small. However, there were also great advantages in the compact house, not the least being its moral virtues. The puritan vicar William Wakely argued that these houses encouraged 'love and the companion-ant marriage because of the shared accommodation of man and wife'. In rambling older houses 'the great personages doe very often disagree in marriage ... for state and pompes sake, they accustome to divide themselves

BELOW *Mount Grace Manor House in the seventeenth century, a typical 'compact house'*

often in houses and table, commonly in chamber and bed.'

The evolution of larger houses was often complicated by the fact that new building work had to work around an earlier house – though wholescale demolition was sometimes resorted to. The common thread running from the Tudor to Victorian period is the provision of more light, more comfort (in the shape of warmer panelled rooms with more fireplaces) and a concerted attempt to relate the house to gardens and landscape. New materials (brick, cylinder glass and plaster) opened up new possibilities in refinement. Visiting became easier, thanks to improvements in transport, spilling over into the whole house; reception rooms came to occupy the entire ground floor and became the focus of the house. Servants could be below, above or to the side, but were certainly elsewhere; bedrooms were above. Only in towns did reception rooms remain on the first floor.

The reality of the nineteenth century is that most of the population lived in urban terraced housing, a peculiarly British phenomenon, which ranged from elegant Georgian terraces in London and provincial towns to back-to-back housing in working-class industrial villages and towns. The preference for rows of individual houses rather than tenements, as in Scotland, or flats, as on the continent, is difficult to explain, as is the uniformity of areas of terraced housing, with very little variation of status within a street or area of streets – each class kept to itself.

So oppressive is the weight of terraced housing on our housing culture that in late twentieth-century housing estates, architects have, as a reaction, studiously detached houses, sometimes by only a tiny gap, so that they qualify for the much vaunted 'detached' status, despite the added expense in construction and the added heat loss in use. The semi-detached house is now perceived as an unsatisfactory compromise. The 'houses built for the heroes' of two world wars are architecturally a disappointment. But in terms of democratising access to well-heated, adequately lit, fully serviced family accommodation – which for many was the perceived need – the

ABOVE *Four storeys of a house in Gray's Inn Road, London, 1853. For the poor in Victorian cities housing conditions created over-crowding, disease and poverty*

transformation has been enormous. Flats have a niche market, but they are inappropriate in a housing culture where there has never been quite the distinction between country and town or even urban and suburban as elsewhere. Continental visitors often comment on how much of England consists of medium-density single- or two-storey housing followed by a parade of shops – a built environment which repeats itself for mile after mile.

ABOVE *Cut-away drawing of a typical Georgian terraced house. The main reception room is on the first floor*

BELOW *Gustave's Doré's evocation of the grim reality of nineteenth-century mass urban housing*

VERNACULAR HOUSING

Vernacular housing (architecture without architects) might be expected to provide a clearer relationship between what people want out of their houses and the social relations they wish their home to demonstrate. People have built their own houses since the Neolithic era, but many self-builders have been constrained by the building materials at hand, shortage of time, the threat of demolition and their disadvantaged position at the bottom of a class system. The results, such as the houses of landless agricultural labourers in the eighteenth and nineteenth century, were often transitory, but unfortunately nineteenth-century observers were not anthropologists and restricted their comments on these houses to their lack of sanitation, overcrowding, dampness and squalor. Regional cultural variations are often limited to materials (cob, turf, stone, etc.), details of construction, such as plaited grass ceilings or wattle chimneys, and the way the house was used; one

of the few exceptions being the Lewis multi-pile black house.

The divide between vernacular and polite architecture varies with the type of house, the size of house, and the period and region in which it was built. For example, the yeoman farmhouses of the Great Rebuilding were vernacular in style, whereas many Georgian farmhouses were built according to a copybook plan inspired by national rather than local taste. The front elevations of these farmhouses had the same classical symmetry as town houses – a central entrance, flanked by windows and, inside, a hall and parlour divided by the central staircase placed opposite the entrance. In some cases, a Georgian facade was simply built onto the front elevation of an earlier building.

At the level of the landless agricultural labourer, houses were truly vernacular, built by the inhabitant and any local, unpaid help the family could muster. Only local materials were

LEFT *Medieval self-build: illustration from the mid-fourteenth century*

LEFT *Much housing in rural areas was built with whatever local material came to hand, such as the cottage interior in this painting by E H Barnes, 1877*

ABOVE *Some self-built homes for those at the bottom of society were of an extremely temporary nature, in a way today seen in shanty-towns in the cities of the developing world.*

available, so building a house was essentially a question of rearranging the natural surroundings: earth, wood, stone, clay, straw, etc., to make a container that could shelter human beings – a reason why vernacular architecture usually blends into its natural surroundings and also a reason why these houses lasted such a short time and reverted so quickly back to the nature they came from. Their inhabitants left no memorial; the houses often had squatter status, built on common land by roadsides. The inhabitants had only the strength of their backs and arms to barter and their homes had few niceties – a doorway was a necessity; a door frame and door were luxuries, as were windows.

Most of these houses were single cell in plan, with thin partitions dividing the internal space. Above there might be an undivided loft, usually reached by ladder; if stairs were provided they used the chimney for support.

In the mid-nineteenth century

a Royal Commission was set up to examine the dire condition of housing in rural areas, made worse by the decline of the tradition of housing single labourers in the farmer's house. A report of 1843 discovered cottages in Dorset that had upwards of ten people living in them, all sleeping in a loft space as little as 10 feet square. The ground floor was often below ground level and damp, if not waterlogged. The misery of these conditions was heightened by the fact that, unlike in prehistory when everyone lived in houses of light construction and undifferentiated space, the inhabitants of these houses would daily pass the prosperous farmhouses of their masters and, beyond, the great houses of polite society and polite architecture, where the novels of Jane Austen unfold.

While many of these Dorset houses were hovels, even from the outside, nineteenth-century commentators in Wales were confronted with the contrast between the neat cottage exterior and the conditions within:

> The great blot upon this country [mid-Wales] is the condition of its cottages. The exteriors sometimes promise well but are deceptive. There is an appearance of neatness in the thatched roof and whitewashed walls which creates at first a favourable impression.... Nothing, however, can be conceived more wretched than the interior of most of these habitations. The cottage is often only one room, which is divided into two compartments, in one of which the cooking is done; the other is used for meals and contains the beds which are simply boxes, and five or six of these box beds are often packed together within the compass of a few square yards. The windows have no apertures; ventilation is supplied by the chimney and the door; the floor is of clay, and in this close damp, dreary hovel are often housed a labourer, his wife and six or eight children.

LEFT *An idealised rural cottage, a popular genre of Victorian painting*

LEFT *Jane Ebbrell, the house-maid at Erddig, aged 87 in 1793, outside her estate cottage*

HOUSES AND MEANING

We take the familiar for granted. Only when writers on housing have had to make huge jumps in time (prehistoric archaeologists) or distance (anthropologists) have they started to consider meaning.

In the Orkney Islands violent storms have, over the last century, uncovered some of the oldest houses in Europe from their long burial in the sand. Stonebuilt, for want of any other material, and in some cases surviving to roof level, these Stone Age houses possess sufficient surviving features (hearths, beds, dressers, openings) to search for meaning in their contextual relationship.

The right-hand side of these houses is given more importance than the left; the right-hand bed is bigger, as is the little storage place above it; the entrance is to the right of the central axis defined by the hearth. The visitor is encouraged by the architecture to move around the house in an anticlockwise direction. Interestingly, the archaeologist Gordon Childe noted earlier in the twentieth century that, in the black houses of the Western Isles, women occupied the left-hand side of the house and men

the right-hand side; guests sat behind the hearth, facing the entrance. The archaeological evidence from the Barnhouse homes in Orkney may confirm the antiquity of this tradition: high phosphate levels (produced, among other things, by urine), may suggest the presence of babies and toddlers on the left-hand side.

The great majority of entrances to Orkney Neolithic houses are on a south-east/north-west axis, as are Orcadian tombs – the houses of the dead. The rectangular hearths at Barnhouse are aligned on the crosslike orientation of midsummer sunrise and sunset, and midwinter sunrise and sunset – peculiar to these latitudes. Archaeologists believe that, as in many traditional cultures, the house represents the cosmos in miniature, and its spatial organisation contains a memory of such things as the seasons of the year, male and female relationships, prohibitions, etc.

One of the houses at Skara Brae, with a female archaeological signature and a door that opened from the outside, has been interpreted as a house

ABOVE *Reconstruction drawing of round houses at Maiden Castle*

ABOVE *Is the combined kitchen/living/eating area the result of the growth of husbands and wives spending more time together?*

RIGHT *Stone built 'furniture' within the homes at Skara Brae, Orkney*

RIGHT *Modern flats that prove that modern housing does not have to be soulless*

FAR RIGHT *The style of mass housing that appears throughout Britain's cities*

for confining women during menstruation, while another house may have been a men's house. Clearly, we have to look far beyond the social framework of our familiar world before we interpret the housing of our distant ancestors. The reluctance of Iron Age populations to move from their round houses to the rectangular Romano-British alternative may be explained in the deeply embedded and reassuring replication of the cosmos and social relations contained in the round house.

The 'civilised' Roman villa could simply be viewed as little more than the provision of comfortable accommodation for rich Roman estate owners. Until comparatively recently, this was how the Roman villa was interpreted. One of the key questions now, however, is why the winged corridor villa did not appear in this part of the Roman Empire until the second century. The corridor, it is argued, acted as the integrative mechanism of the house, controlling and protecting access to other parts of the house and providing an attractive concourse or public zone – many of the corridors are finely tessellated. This change may have coincided with the emergence of Roman Britain as a market economy; many visitors to the villa would be unknown to the occupants and a public zone for introduction and negotiation may have been considered necessary. This is only one interpretation of the corridor villa, but it hangs on the important idea that architecture articulates social relations, in particular those concerning encounter, movement and avoidance.

The corridor in the large Early Modern house, together with the back-stairs, had an entirely different function – to keep the servants out of the way; so the same architectural vocabulary may be used for different purposes and contain different meanings. Modern housing may seem soulless and purely functional, but we must always consider the meaning behind the architecture, whether it is the architect's or builder's vision, or the way the buildings have in fact been used and adapted by the people who live in them.

Many important cultural changes have taken place in the family and in social relations behind the walls of our houses: the gradual erosion of paternalism (employers were less inclined to keep servants, workers or apprentices within their own houses) or the growth of companionate marriage (husband

and wife spending more time together). These changes, which are bound to affect the use of space within a house, are still taking place. Modern commentators argue that our housing will have to provide more accommodation for single parent households and fragmented divorced families with step-children in the future. As well as changes there are also constants; primogeniture in Great Britain, for example, has ensured that, at all levels, few houses were built to accommodate extended families or more than one nuclear family. The 'architecture of privacy' will therefore continue to evolve to meet the pressures of a changing society and balance the demands of change and continuity.

ABOVE *Do high-rise blocks of flats have no meaning?*

BELOW *Regents Park glass extension of 'fragmented family' accomodation*

INDEX

ACKNOWLEDGEMENTS

English Heritage would like to thank:

Peter Dunn, Ivan Lapper, Judith Dobie, Philip Winton and Peter Urmston for permission to reproduce their illustrations

Picture credits:

Advertising Archives back cover and 31cl, 35cl, 41c, 50r, 51cl, 51cr, 51b, cover e, 23r; **AKG** 11b; **Arcaid** 7r, 47bl, 63b, 63tl, 63c; **The Art Archive** 43b, 41tl; **Basle** 43t; **Bibliothèque Arsenal** 24tr; **Birmingham Library Services** 21br; **British Library** (Roy 6EVI f148v) 60t; **Bibliothèque Nationale, Paris**, 22l; **Bridgeman Art Library, London** 6r, 16t, 17l, 25c, 25cl, 27tr, 28bl, 30b, 30t, 32b, 33t, 33cr, 34b, 36tl, 39l, 42tl, 42cr, 45b, 48tl, 50tl, 51t, 52tl, 53t, 55tl, 61t; **Country Life** 35b, 18b; **Embleton** latrine © Frank Graham 24br; **EWA Photos** 47b, 62cr; **Fotomas** 24l, 25t; **Geffrye Museum/John Ronayne** back cover and 13b, 59tr; **Geffrye Museum** 6b, 40b, 49tr; **Highland Folk Museum** 17b; **Hulton/Getty** 9r, 23cl, 23b, 27b, 33b, 35tr, 43c, 45t, 50b, 59b, 61c; **Illustrated London News** 20t; **Kentwell Hall** 31b; **the Marquess of Zetland** 41tr; **Mary Evans Picture Library** cover b, cover d and 19b, 21bl, 23t, 25bl, 25br, 37b,

48b, 48tr, 49tl; **Museum of London** 19tl, 33cl, 36b, 42bl; **Museum of Welsh Life, St Fagans** 17t, 36b; **National Museums of Scotland** 38tl; **National Portrait Gallery** 37t, 47t, 52b; **National Trust** 22b, 22t, 35tl, 39t, 49cr, 49b, 53br, 61b; **Photofusion** 45c; **Rex Features** 13t; **RIBA** 10b, 15b, 59l; **Salisbury Museums** back cover and 42b; **Crown Copyright: Historic Scotland** 12bl, 16l, 40c, 62b, 12bl; **Sothebys** 11t, 54tl, 60b; **St Albans Museums** 32t; **The Tate Gallery** 46b; **Ulster Folk Museum** 28tr; **Victoria and Albert Museum, London** 17r; **Weald and Downland Open Air Museum** 12br, 14t, 27tl, 58t; **Winchester Museum** 44b, **York Museums** 29r, 29t, 30l, 31t, 31cr, 33r, 42cl.

All other photographs are the copyright of **English Heritage** (telephone Photographic Library on 0207 973 3338 for further details).

Every effort has been made to trace the copyright holders and we apologise in advance for any unintentional omission, which we would be pleased to correct in any subsequent edition of this book.